Series Editor **Mike Burghall**

Humanising Your Coursebook

Mario Rinvolucri

Published by
DELTA PUBLISHING
Quince Cottage
Hoe Lane
Peaslake
Surrey GU5 9SW
England

First published 2002
Reprinted 2003, 2006, 2007, 2009

ISBN 0 954198 60 3

Designed by Christine Cox
Cover illustration by Phillip Burrows
Project managed by Chris Hartley
Printed by Halstan & Co Ltd

Acknowledgements
Thank you to the students who have stimulated the creation
of new exercises in response to their specific language needs.

Thank you to Pilgrims network collaborators and colleagues
round the world, people like Luke Prodromou and Herbert
Puchta, Christine Frank and Bonnie Tsai.

Thank you to the wider set of outstanding methodologists
whose technical thought is also found in this book, people
like Paul Seligson.

Thank you to the oral tradition among EFL teachers which
carries exercises constantly from mouth to mouth, often
transforming and improving them in the process.

Thank you to my own masters and guides: Carlos Maeztu,
Lou Spaventa, Bernard Dufeu, Earl Stevick, Caleb Gattegno,
Bandler, Grinder and Dilts, to name but a few.

Finally, thanks to my wife, Sophie, for her permanent
scepticism about the value of my work which forces me to
stay on my toes.

The publishers would like to thank Tanya Whatling for her
valuable editorial contribution.

Preface

I lost practically half my first ELT class in Athens, back in 1964. It was a late evening class, the students were very tired, and I had no idea how to teach English. I hadn't had any training.

While teaching in Cambridge in 1967, my work was revolutionised by Geoffrey Broughton's *Success with English*. This course had a Teacher's Guide that told me how to teach my next lesson, step by step. It explained grammar and phonology to me, so I could then explain them to the students. For a year or two, I taught the *Success with English* lesson plans faithfully, enthusiastically (the students often loved my lessons) ... and relentlessly.

After a couple of years, I needed something different. I needed **new ways** of teaching those texts about Jillian and Martin (and those marvellous Quentin Blake illustrations, like the ones in the Roald Dahl books). I needed a fresh source, a different mindset, to give me alternative ideas to the lesson plans which I had by then 'over-taught'. In fact, I needed *Humanising Your Coursebook*.

While the Teacher's Guide to a coursebook tends to offer the safety of a set sequence of classroom moves, there may come a time when re-teaching the same sequences gets extremely boring. At that point you may find that having *Humanising Your Coursebook* on the table next to your coursebook really helps you to diversify your lesson preparation.

I remember a conversation in the late 80's with an Italian State Secondary colleague:

'Mario, I have taught *Strategies* three times now. I am starting the book with a new class for the fourth time round. The students love it – the listenings and readings are as good as the first time round, but **I am bored**. I know the texts by heart and can predict student reaction. I don't want to change books ... I just somehow want to teach the same material **differently**.'

It's a pity that *Humanising Your Coursebook* wasn't around then. It would have been ideal for that colleague. No one seems to have thought of writing it or publishing it ... until now.

This is the book we were waiting for.

Mario Rinvolucri

At 60, Mario is entering the second half of his EFL career. He has worked in Chile (Valdivia) and Greece (Athens) and since 1974 has taught English and trained teachers at Pilgrims, Canterbury, UK. He edits *Humanising Language Teaching*, Pilgrims' 'webzine' for language teachers, at www.hltmag.co.uk

His publications include:

Mindgame, a grammar and vocabulary teaching CD Rom, with Fletcher de Téllez, Clarity, Hong Kong, 2000.

Ways of Doing, with Davis and Garside, Cambridge, 1999

Letters, with Burbidge, Gray and Levy, Oxford, 1996

More Grammar Games, with Davis, Cambridge, 1995

Dictation, with Davis, Cambridge, 1988

Vocabulary, with Morgan, Oxford, 1986

Grammar Games, Cambridge, 1984

Once Upon a Time, with Morgan, Cambridge, 1983

Using the Mother Tongue, with Dellar, ETp-Delta, 2002

Contents

Introduction

Humanising Your Coursebook

This Book is for You if ...

- you are just off a training course and feel the need to diversify from standard procedures and experiment with new techniques, on the way to establishing your own personal style of teaching.

- you like your current coursebook because it goes down well with the students, but need to do something different with the coursebook material, just to keep yourself sane!

- you have large secondary classes and discipline problems. Many of the suggestions in this book lock the students into 'disciplining' activities. It proposes a variety of methods, and suggests that sometimes discipline problems are a manifestation of student boredom. Variety, in and of itself, can palliate this boredom.

- you are stuck with a coursebook that you and your students find dull. The wide range of proposed techniques will give life even to flat and inappropriate readings and listenings. For example, however unmotivating a text may sound or look, the instruction, 'Choose a couple of words, phrases or sentences you really like' is one that rarely fails. Each student then reads out the word / sentence they like and says why. This is an 85% fail-safe way of dealing with a really boring text. But remember, even this technique can still fail with a rebellious mid-teens class in the last period before lunch!

- you accept that some students need the order and sequence that a coursebook can give, but feel constricted by the lockstep nature of the sequencing. *Humanising Your Coursebook* offers you options so that you can choose, within the confines of the coursebook, techniques that satisfy your need for choice.

- you like teachers' resource books, but find them hard to marry with the coursebook. This book offers you an arranged marriage!

- you no longer use coursebooks. All the techniques in this book are applicable to the texts your students generate and to the texts you select for them, knowing their needs and interests.

What is in This Book

- *Humanising Your Coursebook* is packed with practical activities, many of which are so obvious that people may not have used them in the past. You don't see them because they're right there, under your nose. For example, why not get the students to write their own comprehension questions, which they then put to other students? In writing the questions, they are doing comprehension work. And who knows better than they do what the group does and doesn't understand? Why should coursebook writers or teachers write about things they can't possibly apprehend nearly as well as students can?

- The book has many short activities that you can easily fit into the way you normally teach a coursebook unit. It allows you to try new things, but with a low-risk time span.

- Most activities require minimal preparation, so it is worth scanning *Humanising Your Coursebook* between 8.45 and 9.00 am, if your first class starts at 9.15!

- The book focuses not just on the present coursebook unit – it also previews and revises. If you are on Unit 7, *Humanising Your Coursebook* offers you activities that may take students right to the end of the book or back over some of the previous six units. It invites you to see the coursebook as a whole.

- In these activities, the students are 'centre stage' and you, the teacher, are in the wings. They are doing the speaking, thinking, writing, moving and listening. In some cases, you act as activity model / demonstrator and then they get on with it. In other cases, they plunge straight into the task and you suddenly find you have time to ...
    help individuals
    observe the whole class
    observe groups
    notice your own state of mind / heart
    take a rest.

Some Beliefs

I believe that Neuro-Linguistic-Programming is right:

- people learn through all their senses
- the best way to teach a class is to make sure that the input and the activities are multi-sensory.

Humanising Your Coursebook offers plenty of exercises that include movement, so that kinaesthetic learners are allowed to escape immobility, which is what they most dread and to which they are mostly condemned in class.

I believe that Howard Gardner is right when he writes in *Frames of Mind* (Palladin, Granada Publishing, 1986), that our students come with multiple intelligences, and that good teaching draws on each intelligence (musical, spatial, kinaesthetic, interpersonal and intrapersonal), as well as the 'traditional' intelligences (linguistic and logical-mathematical). *Humanising Your Coursebook* proposes ideas that activate the different intelligences, including the introspective, intrapersonal one, that can get overlooked in very communicative classrooms.

I believe that Caleb Gattegno is right, too, when he says that students:

- learn by paying good attention in the here and now
- learn when their minds are in 'discovery mode'
- learn best when the teacher does the minimum necessary to set them on the right road.

With Gattegno, Gardner and NLP as my thinking guides, I have no excuse for not bringing together a rich swarm of activities for you to use in tandem with your coursebook.

Humanising Your Teaching

What follows is one teacher's way of looking at his students and being with them. It may very well not be the right way for your gender, age, style, energy, or for your idea of who you want to be as a teacher.

My intention is not to prescribe behaviours or beliefs. It is simply an outline of another teacher's positions that may help you become more aware of your own.

The Classroom as a Place

I have colleagues who bring in flowers, who cover the walls with posters, who have music playing before the lesson so the students enter another spatial, acoustic world when they come to class. In these matters I am fairly weak. These are some of the things I do:

- I will, if I can, arrive ten minutes before the start of class and put one or two things up on the board, maybe a thought about the last class, maybe a joke, maybe an instruction for the coming class.

- I may put a reading on the students' chairs so they have something to glance through when they come in.

- I may put an individual reading on one person's chair.

- I decide where in the space of the room I am going to teach from today so that the students then see and feel the space differently.

- In some classes, I write them a group letter each day, and copies of this will go on their seats.

This way each student can come into the 'English space' at their own pace.

Some Behaviours

The teachers' own behaviours have a lot to do with setting the atmosphere in a group. Here are some of mine that I am consciously aware of:

- If I ask the students to read something together silently as a class, I do the same task myself. By joining in, I add to the group's reading energy.

- If we are writing letters to each other round the class, I abandon parent role and join in energetically, sending off six letters to different people round the group to the average student's one. This behaviour frees me of my paternal role, my role as mentor, and offers me to the students as a sibling, an elder brother and a correspondent.

- If the students are doing a writing task where I guess they need help and correction, I ask those who want me to look over their shoulders at my discretion, to put a piece of paper on their tables saying, 'Come over when you like'. I do not go near students without this piece of paper next to them unless they call me over. This teacher behaviour allows independently-minded students to work on their own, while others get the help they feel they need. This sort of behaviour empowers students and offers them autonomy.

- If there is a student's writing or drawing on the board, I always ask the group's permission before erasing it. This public space is one we share.

- If, in a late teenage or adult class, a student interrupts me, I will mentally note where I had got to, and then go with the interruption, to return to my own point later.

Some Skills

What a teacher does in terms of self-management also sets the tone of the class. Here are some of the skills I have tried to develop:

- Stay internally and externally silent while a student is trying to puzzle something out.

- Listen to these aspects of student speech:

    the voice quality text (such as loud / soft, fast / slow, deep / high, etc.)
    the postural and gestural text
    the face muscle text
    the intonational-musical text
    the semantic, linguistic text

    If I manage this five-fold listening, I don't have time to come up with smart responses.

- Give myself time to think before reacting to a student observation or question.

- Vary mood, tempo and own-and-student states of awareness. My best teaching comes with many changes of pace, even within one lesson.

- Be skilful and aware in the use of my own voice, using the whole range of this amazing tool.

- Monitor what the students already know, even if they are unaware of it, and then only to teach the essentials of what they do not yet know.

Some Useful Beliefs and Attitudes

Underlying teachers' classroom behaviours will be a powerful set of beliefs and attitudes. Here are some of mine which I regard as useful:

- My map of a situation in the classroom is not the territory, it is one of thirty often very different mappings in that room. My mapping certainly has no 'objective' status, and, because it is 'primus inter pares', I need to be very careful to examine it critically.

- My pleasure in teaching, and pleasure is central to me, lies in wonderment at the ten, thirty, fifty human universes in front of me. What amazing autobiographies

are sitting on those seats, what amazing ways they have of seeing and feeling the world. Look at Eleni, she dreams in technicolour, while I dream in vague black and white. Look at Bartok, he told me that he can see all our auras each morning ... extraordinary!

- I create my 'good students' in my head and also my 'bad students'. This mental moralising is very natural, laughably constrictive and surrealistically dysfunctional. I believe I need to stand right outside these odd ways of thinking.

- There is no failure and no success, only feedback.

- When I teach English, I teach myself. The students are learning the language, but it is inextricably bound up with 'marioishness'. I need to learn more about this 'marioishness'.

- Anything a student or colleague does at a particular moment is the best behaviour possible within their way of seeing things. This goes for all of Monir's loudness, lack of discipline, wool-gathering and teenage need to dominate, though he is chronologically twenty-five years old.

- It is right to enjoy the power that awareness of people gives me in my classroom and among my colleagues.

An Invitation

And finally, if:

- you have comments about this book or good, technical ideas and would like to share them, you might like to contact me.

    Mario Rinvolucri
    Pilgrims
    Orchard Street
    Canterbury CT2 8BF
    UK
    mario@pilgrims.co.uk

- you want to see your ideas up on the Web, then *Humanising Language Teaching*, Pilgrims' 'webzine' for teachers, is the place.

    www.hltmag.co.uk

1

Icebreakers and Warm-up Activities

In my experience it is hard to overestimate the importance of a 'warm-up'. It makes no difference if you have a packed syllabus waiting to be taught. Time and again I have finished a course and felt that I should have done a lot more warm-up and group formation activity on the first day or two. With hindsight, I can see just how much time would have been saved by warming the students up better at the start of the course. I have often been over-eager to get into 'proper language content'.

Musicians tune their instruments up, athletes never sprint until their bodies are prepared, people in a choir do vocal exercises before singing. Our students, too, need to warm into both the target language and being in their group.

A brief investment here brings huge dividends in terms of energy released, anxiety calmed and the linguistic unconscious opened up and made ready to go.

Filling a Foot

Level	elementary to advanced
Materials	sheets of paper

1 Pair the students and ask them to take off their shoes. Ask them to place a sheet of paper on the floor and draw round their partner's foot. They then 'fill' the foot outline with information about the partner, **excluding** name, age and country (if this is an international class).

If drawing round a foot would be either embarrassing or taboo, get the students to draw round each other's hands.

2 Collect the sheets and shuffle them. Hand them out at random. No one should get their own sheet.

3 Tell the students to find the owner of the foot on their sheet and get lots more information to put inside the shape. They add the name of the owner of the outline.

4 Put the sheets up round the walls of the classroom.

Acknowledgement: I learnt this icebreaker from John Carthy, who teaches on Pilgrims children's courses.

What Does Your Voice Look Like?

Level	elementary to advanced
Materials	none

1 Get the students to sit or stand in a large circle.

2 Ask every second student to stand in the centre of the circle. If you have an odd number, one student stays out of the game and observes.

3 Tell the students left in the circle they will be closing their eyes in a moment. The people from the centre will approach them and have an initial conversation, like one you might have on a plane or train.

4 The task of the 'blind' person is to get an idea of what the other speaker is like **physically**. The 'sighted' students time the conversation to three minutes. At the end of this time, the 'blind' students describe their interlocutor **before** opening their eyes.

5 After this first round, allow time for feedback, first from the 'blind' and then the 'sighted' students.

6 Repeat the activity the other way round. The blind become the sighted and vice versa. Again, give time for feedback.

Acknowledgement: I learnt this exercise ten years ago from Elayne Phillips, one of the Bell School's best teacher trainers in the 80's and early 90's.

Variation
1 Tell the students to talk to one other person for a couple of minutes, introducing themselves.

2 Tell the partners to move across the room, away from each other. Ask the students to continue talking, without saying who they are. The partners shut their eyes and come back towards each other, trying to recognise each other by the voice alone.

3 Get the students to take new partners and repeat the exercise. Allow four to six 'rounds'.

Acknowledgement: This exercise was first proposed in an ELT context by the late 70's coursebook, *All's Well* (Sagot and Dickinson, Didier).

Who Are You?

Level   elementary to lower intermediate
Materials   sheets of paper / notebooks

1 Get the students to brainstorm all the family relationships they can think of: cousin, mother-in-law, uncle, etc.

2 Tell the class something about yourself in terms of family relationships. For example:

I'm X's cousin
I'm Y's brother.

3 Ask them to take down what you say and then build a partial family tree for your family.

4 Tell the students something more about yourself, using this structure repeatedly:

I'm a woman / man who ...

5 Pair the students. Student A asks their partner, 'Who are you?' ten to twenty times. Student B gives different answers each time.

6 Get the students to repeat the same activity the other way round.

Whose Story is It?

Level   lower intermediate to advanced
Materials   none

Preparation
Tell your students to come ready to tell a personal story / anecdote in the **next** lesson. Ask them to prepare to **tell** it in English. It is better if they don't write it out.

1 In the next lesson, group the students in threes if you have a small class and in sixes with a larger class. Ask each student to tell their story to the other students in their group.

2 Ask the students to prepare to tell **one** of the group's stories to the whole class. The students from outside the group will have to guess whether the storyteller is recounting their own story or the story of someone else in the group and, if so, who.

3 The first group's storyteller tells their story, followed by the other groups telling their stories.

Acknowledgement: I was taught this technique by a teacher trainee at Pilgrims. She had learnt it four years previously from Sheelagh Deller, a Pilgrims faculty colleague.

Questions to Myself

Level	lower intermediate to advanced
Materials	sheets of paper

1 Ask the students to think about a sport, hobby or outside interest they have and write twenty questions addressed to themselves, the answers to which might interest another person.

2 Suppose the subject is canoeing, the question, 'Do I have a canoe?' is boring if the answer is simply 'Yes'. But it may be interesting if the answer is 'Well, no, because my parents think it's a risky sport.'

3 Give the students about twenty minutes to write their questions and push them towards writing a full twenty. They are likely to complain that twenty are too many!

4 Pair students and ask them to exchange questionnaires. Student A should ask student B the questions that student B originally wrote to him/herself, changing the grammar.

5 The students then work the other way round, with student B asking student A to answer student A's own questions.

Variation

Pair students who have written questions about similar areas of interest. Student A puts their **own** questions to student B, and vice versa.

Acknowledgement: I am pretty sure I learnt this exercise in 1979 from Carlos Maeztu, who had in turn learnt it from *Caring and Sharing in the Foreign Language Classroom* (Moskowitz G, Newbury House, 1978).

Name-learning Multiplication

Level	elementary to lower intermediate
Materials	none

1 Ask the students to sit in circles of twelve to fifteen. If you have fixed furniture, then have the students stand in circles.

2 Ask one of them to say their name loudly and clearly to the group and a multiplication they like. For example:

I'm Roxana and I am 4 x 5.

3 This student chooses another member of the group who has to introduce him / her and then go on to introduce themselves:

She's Roxana and she is 4 x 5, and I am Manolo and I am 7 x 7.

4 This student picks a third student, who introduces the first two and then themselves. Writing is not allowed. If you have a 'normal' sized class of forty-five students, then the three groups will be doing the exercise simultaneously.

Variations

a Ask students to be letters of the alphabet:

I'm Michiko and I am an 'x'.

b Ask students to be containers:

I'm Mario and I'm an ashtray.

c Ask students to be sea animals:

I'm Thierry and I'm a squid.

d Ask students to be parts of a car:

I'm Gerhard and I'm the clutch.

Talking to a Puppet

Level	beginner to advanced
Materials	toilet roll cores (at least one per student), scissors, glue, corks, sheets of coloured paper and coloured pens

1 Ask each student to make a puppet that represents their present mood. They can take all the time they need.

2 Working individually, the students introduce themselves to their puppet and they get the puppets to introduce themselves in their turn.

3 Tell students to have a 'yesterday' conversation with the puppet, based on one of the moods the student was in yesterday.

4 Now get the students to think forward to their next happy event and to have a conversation with the puppet just before that event.

5 Get the group up and moving around: the puppets meet each other and talk about their past lives.

6 Put the puppets up round the walls of the room and have a general feedback discussion.

Variation

With mature business English classes ask students to make puppets to represent people in their office. They have dialogues with these people in front of the class.

NOTES: This activity is **not** recommended for lower secondary classes, but works excellently with kindergarten, primary, upper-secondary students and adults.

Puppets are also very useful in a one-to-one situation, as they fill the room with people relevant to the student and his life.

Acknowledgement: Denise Özdeniz presented this technique during a methodology workshop at Pilgrims in the summer of 2000.

Breathing Sentences Out

Level	beginner to lower intermediate
Materials	none

1 Get the students to stand up and breathe in to a count of two, and breathe out to a count of two. Do this eight or nine times.

2 Now tell them to breathe in to a count of four, and breathe out to a count of four. Do this several times.

3 Now tell them to breathe in to a count of four and give them a short sentence to say as they breathe out. This could be one taken from the coursebook or from a student's composition. For example:

John went to the party

4 Tell them to repeat the original sentence each time they breath out, adding a phrase. For example:

John went to the party **given by Mary**.
(breathe in four)
John went to the party given by Mary **in London**.

NOTE: Standing up and doing breathing work wakes a class up. Oxygen helps learning, and breathing in rhythm binds a group together.

Acknowledgement: Luke Prodromou presented this exercise in *IATEFL Issues*, No. 154, April / May 2000.

2

Grammar

This section gives you ideas for revisiting key areas in your coursebook without repeating the activities that are in it. *Ready Made* deals with the teaching of specific grammar points. Scan through and cross-reference with your coursebook for easy use. *Make it to Measure* offers you activities which you can use with virtually any grammar content at different levels.

From Home to School / Work

Level	lower intermediate to advanced
Materials	sheets of paper / notebooks

1 Draw your own route from home to class on the board.

2 Write in some prepositional phrases along the route. For example:

- through the wood
- under the railway line
- over the river
- up the hill
- round the roundabout
- left at the crossing
- over the level crossing

3 Write in some verbs phrases along the route, too:

- I leave home
- I go down the hill
- I cross the road
- I run
- I dawdle
- I speed up
- I turn right
- I go straight on

4 Ask the students to draw their own route from home to school or work and then add in prepositional phrases and verb phrases.

5 Pair students and ask them to describe their route to their partner.

6 Ask the students to write half a page describing their partner's route to school or work.

Variation

Ask your students to view their route from a different perspective, for example, from the perspective of a bird flying at a height of ten metres.

Acknowledgement: This idea comes from the work of Marcial Boo.

Prepositions for My Drawing

Level	elementary to lower intermediate
Materials	sheets of paper, plenty of coloured pencils or equivalent for each student

1 Dictate the following list of words:

cloud	door
snow	river
rain	mountain
rice field	man
sun	woman
tree	snake
car	dog
house	cat
window	

2 Ask each student to make a colour drawing, including all of the above items, in a coherent landscape.

3 Pair the students and ask them to sit back to back.

4 One partner has to accurately describe their picture to the other, who should try to draw it, using the correct colours. The students should produce sentences like:

- There's a blue mountain in the middle at the top.
- The orange sun is half behind the mountain.
- Below the mountain there's a yellow house.

Circulate, helping the students use prepositions accurately.

5 When one student has finished their description, they compare the dictated picture and the original.

6 Ask the students to work the other way round.

7 Get the students to shout out the prepositions they have used and write them up on the board.

Acknowledgement: I read this idea in an article by Rod Gottula, in *The Language Teacher*, Japan, August 2000.

Throwing Prepositions

Level	elementary to lower intermediate
Materials	none

1 Get the students to sit in a circle.

2 Throw a ball to one of the students, saying, 'From (your name) to (student's name) for (name of second student).' For example:

From Mario to Keiko for Ahmed.

3 Keiko then throws the ball to Ahmed. Ahmed then starts the sequence again:

From Ahmed to Stig for Hayal

4 Use these patterns with the throwing of the ball:
  - From A to B via C.
  - From A to B under C.
  - From A to B over C.
  - From A to B behind C.
  - From A to B around C three times.
  - From A to B through C. (The students arch their arms forward so the ball can be passed 'through' them.)
  - From A to the person between B and C.
  - From A to the person on B's right.
  - From someone in yellow to someone with blue shoes.
  - From A to B for someone who ... ('has' + past participle).

Spatial Prepositions

Level	elementary to lower intermediate
Materials	none

1 When you want to give the students freer practice of spatial prepositions, put them in threes and then demonstrate with a volunteer, giving between a dozen and twenty answers:

Student: Where do you live?
You: In this country.
Student: Where do you live?
You: Not far from here.
Student: Where do you live?
You: In a house with red windows.

2 The groups start working:
  - Student A asks 'Where do you live?' over and over again.
  - Student B gives a different answer each time.
  - Student C notes down each of student B's answers.

3 Give the student C's a chance to read out any answers they guess are wrong. The class can correct them.

4 Repeat the activity twice so that everybody has been observer, questioner and answerer.

Not Yours, Mine!

Level	elementary
Materials	none

1 Write these words on the board:

mine   hers   yours
ours   his   theirs   its
yes   no   not

2 Invite a volunteer to come out and do an impromptu dialogue with you in front of the class, using only the above words, something like this:

You: His? His?
Volunteer: Not his! Mine!
You: Yours? Yours? Not yours. Ours!
Volunteer: No, not ours. Mine! Mine! Mine!

3 Pair the students and ask them to use the same set of words in simultaneous dialogues.

4 Invite two or three pairs who feel like it to perform their dialogues in front of the whole class.

Variation
You can get the same sort of dialogue going with any set of vocabulary:

- pan, dish, knife, colander, spoon , ladle
- January, February, March
- modem, mouse, VDU, disk

Acknowledgement: I learnt this technique from Gracia Rodríguez, in an ESADE workshop in Barcelona.

Personal Pronoun Riddles

Level	elementary
Materials	sheets of paper / notebooks

1 Give the class this riddle to solve:

It has two wheels.
It has no motor.
It has a saddle.

They should get 'bike' pretty fast.

2 Pick something that is common to several people in the group, for example, a skirt, and say:

Maria ... hers is blue.
Mine is green.
Jane and Gabriella ... theirs are red.

(You are referring to the colours of real skirts worn by people in the group.) The students have to solve the riddle and come up with the word 'skirt'.

3 Ask the students to write three riddles about things owned by people in the group, using three personal pronouns according to the same pattern. Remind them of 'mine', 'ours', 'yours', 'his', 'hers' and 'theirs'. The three things may be things visible in the room or, if the students know each other well, they may things they have at home (for example, pets, etc.).

4 Group the students in sixes to read out their riddles and solve them.

Acknowledgement: I learnt this technique from Susan Morris, writing in *MELTA News*, N° 38, June 1999. She writes that she adapted the technique from *English Elements*, Hueber Verlag.

Guessing Other People's Frequency

Level	elementary to lower intermediate
Materials	slips of paper

1 Put 'I always ...' at the top of the board and 'I never ...' at the bottom.

2 Ask the students to provide the adverbs of frequency that go in between. Ask where each one should go in relation to the others.

3 Group the students in sixes and ask each one to write their name on a slip of paper that is then folded and collected by one student in each group. The names are then given out so no one gets their own name.

4 Go round, saying to different students:

You used to be Giulia - who are you now?

5 Tell the students to write one sentence, in the role of the person whose name they have got, for each adverb of frequency. It must be a sentence that describes a supposed habit of the person.

6 When the students have written their sentences, ask one person in each group to start like this:

I am Sau Ying. I always go to the market on Sunday morning.

7 Sau Ying then has right of reply. They can correct the information within the prescribed structure:

No, I **sometimes** go, not **always**.

8 The student who said, 'I am Sau Ying.' then reads out the second sentence, which the real Sau Ying corrects, and so on.

9 Sau Ying then reads out her sentences about another group member, and is corrected when wrong. This oral work goes on in the groups of sixes simultaneously.

NOTE: You can use this activity to 'carry' a wide variety of structures.

Comparing Myself with Others

Level	elementary to lower intermediate
Materials	sheets of paper / notebooks

1 Elicit from the students the comparative structures they have met in the coursebook and write them up on the board.

2 Group the students in eights.

3 Ask every student to write seven sentences, each sentence comparing themselves with a different member of the group. For example:

Keiko has longer hair than me.
I am nearly as tall as Gustav.
Perhaps I'm as careful as Anouk.

Circulate, helping with the grammar.

4 When the writing is over, ask the students in each group of eight to pick one name and read out all the sentences about this person. Continue with the second person, and so on.

NOTE: Don't use this exercise if you consider there are strong tensions between the students or if you have some marginalised students.

Picture Negation:
There is / There are

Level	elementary to lower intermediate
Materials	notebooks

1 Ask a student with a good hand and eye to draw a picture on the board, including a lot of things that have recently been named in your coursebook: words like 'cars', 'garden', 'dogs', 'shop', 'tree', 'spoons', etc . Ask your Picasso to draw one example of some items and several examples of the others.

2 Teach the class the phrase:

There is ...
There are some ... in the picture.

3 Ask the students to make sentences about the picture, using these patterns.

4 Now teach these patterns:

There is no (uncountable) ... in the picture.
There aren't any ...
X's gone. X've gone.

5 The students come up to the board and rub out one thing or category of thing, saying:

There is no rain in the picture.	**or**
There are no trees in the picture.	**or**
The tree's gone.	**or**
The trees've gone.	

6 Once the board is clear, invite the students to come and write the words in the place where the object was before.

7 The students copy this 'word picture' down.

NOTE: This activity teaches 'there is' and 'there are', which you would expect at beginner level, and previews the present perfect. Constant previewing and revising help learning. For students from non-Indo-European languages, this exercise is also powerful practice with the use of the definite article.

Acknowledgement: The idea of talking about what is not there comes from *Grammar Practice Activities* (Ur P, Cambridge 1988).

Likes, Hates and the Gerund

Level	elementary to lower intermediate
Materials	sheets of paper / notebooks

1 Ask the students to draw six concentric circles on paper. Tell them to put their name in the central circle and the names of half a dozen family members, friends or acquaintances in the other circles. If the person is close to them, they put their name in an inner circle, and if they are more distant, in an outer circle.

2 Ask the students to think about each person and write two sentences: one about what the person likes them doing and one about what the person hates them doing. For example:

Bruno likes me leaving him in peace.
Bruno hates me talking too loud in public.

3 Group the students in fours to say who their people are and to share their sentences.

Asking Questions

Level	elementary to upper intermediate
Materials	notebooks

Preparation
Choose a unit with a good story in it from the end of the coursebook, or a story from the listening cassettes from way ahead.

1 Pick out three to four semi-key words (often full key words give the story away completely) and put these on the board, without saying where they come from.

2 Tell the students the words come from a story. If they want to find out what the story is about, they should ask you 'Yes' / 'No' questions.

3 If they get stuck in their questioning, give them a clue and ask them each to write two questions. Wander round the class and help the weaker students. Take questions first from the quieter ones.

4 Once the students have got the outline of the story, ask them to check it by going forward to the listening or reading passage in question.

Interrupting the Coursebook

Level	lower intermediate to advanced
Materials	none

Preparation
This is an activity for when you come towards the end of your coursebook. For homework, ask one of the more extrovert students to prepare to tell one of the narrative texts from near the beginning of the book.

1 In the next lesson, tell the narrator-student that they are going to tell the story from that unit to the class. Tell the other students that it is their job to try to stop him telling it, by asking as many questions about his text as they possibly can, like this:

Narrator: Well, this sea captain ...
Student 1: How old was he?
Narrator: About fifty and he took his ship into ...
Student 2: What colour was the ship?
Narrator: Blue. The captain ...
Student 3: Did he have a wife?
Narrator: More than one, and as I was saying, he took his ship ...

2 Get the telling / questioning started and take note of interrogative forms used incorrectly.

3 At the end of the exercise, write the incorrect interrogatives up on the board and ask the class to come up with their own corrections of them. Don't help them. The students almost always know, if they take the time to think.

Miming Third Person Singular, Present Simple

Level	beginner to elementary
Materials	none

1 Demonstrate the activity with a volunteer. Ask the volunteer to think of a person whose habits they know very well. Now ask them to show you some of this person's habits in mime. Neither you nor the volunteer speak during the miming. Now you mime the habits of a person you know very well.

2 In pairs and in silence, the students mime the actions of a person they know really well. Give them three minutes each way.

3 Pair the pairs and ask the students to verbally describe what they have understood about their partner's person's habits. Make it clear on the board that they will need to use the '-s' and '-es' of the third person singular, present simple. Go round the classroom, helping with vocabulary.

4 Do a vocabulary round-up of new verbs they have needed to use on the board.

How Simple is the Past?

Level	elementary to lower intermediate
Materials	sheets of paper / notebooks

Preparation
When you have completed a couple of units that introduce irregular simple past forms, go back to one of the listening or reading passages in the coursebook and pull out all the past tense verbs, regular and irregular.

1 Ask the students to quickly re-read the passage.

2 Tell them to shut their books and invite one of them to the board to copy down the verbs you now dictate, **out of their order in the passage**. All the students take them down and you correct the work of the person at the board.

3 Group the students in threes and ask them to decide on the order of the verbs in the passage, numbering them.

4 Ask one student to come to the board and suggest the numbers agreed by their group. Don't interfere. Allow the students to disagree with the person at the board. The less you say, the stronger the technical discussion may get.

5 The students open their books and check the correct order of the verbs.

NOTE: The ideal text for this exercise is a good story from the coursebook cassette, or one you tell the class yourself. **Listening** for the verb orders really helps fix them as sound entities in the students' minds.

Contrasting Present Perfect and Past Simple

Level	elementary to upper intermediate
Materials	none

1 Sit with your students in a big circle. If you can't do this because of fixed furniture, then make a standing circle.

2 Place an empty chair next to you. Say to the group, 'If anyone has been to ... come and sit / stand next to me.' (You could use the name of a town in the students' country, or the name of a foreign country.)

3 Now ask the student who comes to the empty chair two questions:

You: When did you go there?
Student: I went...
You: Where exactly did you go?
Student: I went to..., I stayed in ...

4 The student who is now next you has left an empty space somewhere else in the circle. One of the students either side of the new empty space starts the sequence again:

If anybody had been to ... come and sit / stand next to me.

Run the exercise at a brisk pace and stop before the students lose interest.

Building Houses: Past Perfect

Level	lower to upper intermediate
Materials	sheets of paper / notebooks

When you have exhausted the possibilities in the coursebook, this activity can be used to teach the tense sequences.

1 Dictate these sentences to the students:

- They built the walls.
- They cleared the ground.
- They laid the drains.
- They put in the electrics.
- They plastered the walls inside.
- They dug foundation trenches.
- They poured cement into the trenches.
- They put up the rafters.
- They tiled the roof.
- They painted the inside walls.
- They put in the plumbing.
- They agreed the plans with the client.
- They laid grass round the new house.

Check that they understand and can spell all the words.

2 Ask the students to work in pairs and put the sentences in a logical sequence, re-writing them like this:

When they had agreed the plans with the client, they cleared the ground.
When they had cleared the ground, they dug the foundation trenches.

3 Get different pairs to read out their sequences. There is likely to be some disagreement.

Acknowledgement: Gerlinde Wisiol uses this technique with her senior secondary school students in Munich.

Irregular Verb Card Game

Level	elementary to lower intermediate
Materials	sixty small, blank cards for each group of students.

1 Group students in fives and give out sixty blank cards to each group.

2 Select twenty irregular verbs that you want the students to work on and get them look up the irregular verb table in their coursebook. Ask the students to copy these twenty verbs (one verb part per card) onto the playing cards.

3 Demonstrate the game with one of the groups:

- Shuffle the verb cards and deal thirty of them, putting the rest face down as 'card pool' on the table.
- Student A looks through their hand to try to find an infinitive. If they find one, they lay it down face up. If not, they have to take a card from the pool.
- Student B either places the simple past of the infinitive that Student A has laid down on the table or starts a new verb set with a new infinitive.
- The first student to complete a verb set by laying down a past participle takes the completed set.
- At end of play, the student with the most completed sets is the winner.

4 Gather in the cards to play with the next class who need to practise irregular verbs.

Acknowledgement: This game was devised by Margot Schauer between day 2 and day 3 of an INSET workshop for secondary teachers in Munich, in the spring of 2000.

Rhythmical Irregular Verbs

Level	elementary to lower intermediate
Materials	none

1 To practise a set of twenty or so irregular verbs, ask the students to stand up and demonstrate with 'go - went - gone'.

- You and the students touch your ankles and say 'go'.
- You touch your hips and say 'went'.
- You fling your arms above your head and say 'gone'.

2 Now take the verb 'cut'. This time you and the students touch your ankles three times, chanting 'cut - cut - cut'.

3 With the verb 'teach' you touch your ankles once and your hips twice chanting, 'teach - taught - taught'.

4 Run through all your verbs as rhythmically as you can.

Acknowledgement: I learnt this technique from Gerlinde Wisiol, a teacher trainer at the Munich City INSET Centre.

What I'd Do if ...

Level	lower to upper intermediate
Materials	sheets of paper / notebooks

1 Ask each student to choose someone more powerful than them (a teacher, a parent, a boss, an elder sibling, etc.) and write down ten words to describe this person.

2 Divide the board in two, heading one side 'positive' and the other 'negative'.

3 Ask each student to write up two words on the positive side and two on the negative.

4 Clear the board and put up these sentence stems:
- If I were A, I'd ...
- If I were A, I don't think I would ...
- In A's shoes, I would / I wouldn't ...
- In their position, would I ... ?
- If I was them, well, I guess I'd ...

5 Tell the students to write about ten sentences using the sentence stems on the board about A, their chosen person.

6 In groups of four, the students compare the authority figures they have chosen and the sentences they have written.

Acknowledgement: This exercise first appeared in *Grammar in Action Again* (Frank C, Prentice Hall, 1987).

Thank God it Didn't Happen

Level	upper intermediate to advanced
Materials	none

After students have worked through exercises on unreal conditionals, this activity offers a more personal approach.

1 Prepare to tell the students a near-miss story about something bad that very nearly happened to you but, thank God, did not. End your story with a relieved, 'third conditional' punch line, like:

That coconut would have smashed my head in, if mother hadn't shouted for me to come inside.

2 Tell your story and write the punch line at the very top of the board.

3 Ask if anyone else can tell the class a near-miss story. Invite one student to tell their story. Help them with any words they are short of and write these at the bottom of the board. Help them to produce their own third conditional punch line.

4 Do the same with one more volunteer.

5 Put students in groups of four and ask each person to tell a near-miss story. Go round, helping with vocabulary and with getting the punch lines right.

6 All the students who have told stories write their punch lines on the board. The class corrects any that are grammatically wrong. Let the students do this as best they can.

7 Ask if anybody would like to hear the story behind any of the punch lines. Two or three students tell their stories to the whole class.

Where Can I Add a Word?

Level	elementary to upper intermediate
Materials	none

1 Take a simple sentence from the coursebook that contains the structure you are teaching. Write it up on the board, putting broad spaces between the words.

2 Insert a 'caret' [^] randomly at some point in the sentence, and ask the students to supply an extra word (or two words) to go in at that point. It may be that an addition to the sentence at this point is impossible. Let them find this out.

As I was walking ^ home yesterday, I met Susan.

3 If an extra word can be added, write it in. Ask the student who proposed it to read the whole of the expanded sentence.

4 Continue the activity, putting carets in every position including to the left of the sentence and to the right.

Acknowledgement: This activity comes from the Silent Way, and the less you talk while running it, the better. Your silence leaves the student time for thought and grammatical appropriation.

Oral Sentence Expansion

Level	elementary to lower intermediate
Materials	none

1 Choose a sentence that contains the grammar you are teaching. Get one student to say it and then get the class to chorus it.

2 Explain that you want them to expand the sentence by one word or two. They can put the new word(s) where they like, but with each expansion the sentence must remain a complete sentence. The student proposing the expansion must say the complete new sentence. An expansion sequence might go like this:

Do you like coffee?
Do you like English coffee?
Do you and Kanoko like English coffee?
Do you and Kanoko like English coffee habits?
Why do you and Kanoko like English coffee habits?
Why don't you and Kanoko like English coffee habits?

Change a Letter, Change the Meaning

Level	lower intermediate to advanced
Materials	sheets of paper / notebooks

Preparation
Choose four sentences that carry the structure(s) taught in the current unit of your coursebook.

1 Write the first sentence up on the board and show how you can change the meaning by changing, adding or subtracting **one letter**. For example, for the present perfect continuous sentence, 'Who's been eating my porridge?', here are possible meaning changes:

Who's <u>h</u>eating my porridge?
Who's <u>s</u>een eating my porridge?
Who's been eatin<u>'</u> my porridge?

2 Ask students to decide which of the new sentences show the biggest meaning change from the original. (I'd say one of the first two, but find it hard to choose.)

3 Write the second structure-carrying sentence on the board and ask them, in pairs, to try deleting, substituting or adding a letter.

4 Get students to come and put up a selection of their modified sentences on the board.

5 Check that all the transformations are good English. Then ask the students to put the utterances in order according to how much the meaning has changed. Given the sentence, 'Now they love their neighbours', which of these transformations changes the meaning most strongly?

Ow, they love their neighbours.
No, they love their neighbours.
Now they love their neighbours.
Now! Hey! Love their neighbours!
Now, the love their neighbours ...

6 Repeat the steps above with the next two structure-bearing sentences.

NOTE: As the learners play with English ways of meaning, they are unconsciously imbibing the grammar. Play is central to fast, effective language learning and passing tests.

Shrinking Sentences

Level	elementary to advanced
Materials	none

Preparation
Choose a pattern sentence from the coursebook that exemplifies the structure you are teaching. 'Fatten' the sentence with extra words, so that it is twice or three times its original length.

1 Write your sentence up on the board and tell the students they are going to reduce this sentence to perhaps one word.

2 Tell the students to shout out one word (or two consecutive words) that they want you to take out. Take these out, **even if you know** their excision is impossible grammatically. Ask the proposing student to read the resultant sentence.

If the sentence minus the one or two words is grammatically and syntactically correct, then ask the class for the next reduction. If the sentence is wrong, ask the whole class what they think. If no one is sure, simply write the words back in.

3 Continue in this way until you consider there is no way the sentence can be reduced further.

NOTE: With upper intermediate or advanced students, allow them to take out one, two or even **three** consecutive words.

Variation
Students can also simultaneously shrink and expand sentences.

1 Write up a sentence on the board. Leave broad spaces between the words.

2 Tell the students to try to take out a word somewhere in the sentence and to replace it with **two or three words**. A student who thinks they can do this comes to the board, rubs out the word, and writes in two or three words to replace it. The student then reads the resultant sentence out loud to check if the changes are OK.

3 Stop the exercise before the shrinking-expanding sentence gets too unwieldy.

Diminishing Dialogues

Level	elementary to upper intermediate
Materials	sheets of paper

Preparation
Take a coursebook dialogue and choose a line spoken by one character and the other person's response to it. Tailor both utterances to be seven words long and write these up on the board.

1 Pair the students. Student A takes a sheet of paper and writes down the first sentence. Student B takes another sheet and writes down the second one (as in the first lines of the example below).

2 Ask the students to exchange papers. Student A has to freely respond to the sentence B has given, using a **six**-word sentence. Student B does the same. They work simultaneously.

3 The pair exchange papers again. Student A's response must be in **five** words and student B's, too. They continue in this way until they get down to **one** word.

4 Ask three or four pairs round the class to read aloud both their dialogues, each reading the part they wrote.

Here is an example of a pair of parallel, diminishing dialogues (the first, seven-word lines are taken from a coursebook):

	A	B
7	Oh, sorry, I thought you said furniture.	OK, but can I see the manager?
6	I did. Have you any chairs?	I'm the manager. Can I help?
5	Sorry, we have no chairs.	I want to replace this.
4	Oh dear, no chairs?	Well, it looks dirty ...
3	All sold yesterday	It's completely new.
2	All gone?	It's filthy.
1	Sorry ...	Filthy?!

Variation
Start with one-word utterances and expand up to seven.

Acknowledgement: I learnt this technique in an NLP re-languaging workshop, led by Christina Hall.

Pattern Sentences Backwards

Level	elementary to upper intermediate
Materials	sheets of paper / notebooks

Preparation
Select seven pattern sentences from the coursebook that contain the grammar of this particular unit and write them down.

1 Tell the students you are going to dictate seven sentences to them, but backwards.

2 Dictate the first sentence, 'I have lived here for three years.' but do it backwards:

years three for here lived have I

3 Tell the students to rewrite it in the correct order.

4 Dictate the second sentence and so on, until the seventh.

5 Divide the class into two groups and ask them to read out the sentences chorally. Ask group A to read the first sentence forward, and group B to read the same sentence backwards.

6 Take the students through the sentences at different speeds and different volumes several times.

NOTE: This Gurdjieff-inspired exercise is particularly good if you have dyslexic learners in your class.

A Haughty-Humble Grammar Drill

Level	lower intermediate to advanced
Materials	none

1 Line up nine students in front of the class and give them these roles:

King	Butler
Queen	Guard
Duke	Maid
Knight	Chimney sweep
Jester	

2 Ask them to take on these social roles and walk around, showing who they think they are.

3 Ask them to line up again in status order. The other students get up and approach the 'status people' in the line with the first half of a structure, such as: 'If I were you ...' The status person addressed completes the sentence with '... I'd have a haircut.' The status person has to complete the utterance with the appropriate voice, posture and gesture. They do not vary the words '... I'd have a haircut.'

4 Stop when all the students have had a chance to address each of the status people.

5 Give the students a new sentence and have a new line of status people. Play again as before.

6 Play three or four times with different sentences and different status people.

NOTE: By focusing on the social roles, students are led away from consciously focusing on the grammar structure - it embeds in their minds without arousing their defences.

Acknowledgement: Mike Meston showed this technique to group of colleagues at Pilgrims in the summer of 2000.

I Have Often ...

Level	lower intermediate to advanced
Materials	slips of paper (one for each student) and notebooks

1 Group the students in fives or sixes.

2 Ask them each to write their name on a slip of paper and fold it over. One person takes the slips and shuffles them. Each person in the group takes a slip, making sure it is not their own. They must now take on the identity of the person whose name they have picked.

3 Write these sentence stems up on the board:

- Long ago, I used to ...
- I have often ...
- I have never ...
- Three years ago, I ... (+ simple past)
- These days, I often ...
- Next month, I hope ...
- By this time next year, I'll've ...

4 Working in their new identity, each student completes these sentence stems about 'themselves'.

5 The groups work simultaneously. Student A in the group says, 'I am Juan. Long ago, I used to bully my little brother.' The real Juan then has right of reply and can tell student A something he really did. Student A then goes on, 'I have often been skiing.' The real Juan can reply again. When student A has finished all the sentences, Juan says, 'I am Tomioko ...'

6 Allow time for feedback on how students felt during the writing and the reading out phases.

Acknowledgement: There is a similar exercise in *Grammar in Action Again* (Frank C, Prentice Hall, 1987).

Dictogloss

Level	lower intermediate to advanced
Materials	sheets of paper / notebooks

Preparation

Choose a fairly long sentence from the coursebook that has in it the grammar you are working on. It should have at least some sub-clauses. At upper intermediate level you would need a sentence of this complexity:

> If the conditions had been better, if the money had been right, and if the way forward had seemed brighter, this group of managers would probably not have decided to break away and set up their own company.

1 Tell the students you are going to read them the sentence **once and once only**. Their task is to listen without writing anything and, once you have finished, immediately jot down the key words. From these, they will have to reconstruct the sentences with word-for-word accuracy.

2 Read the sentence clearly and rhythmically. When they have jotted down the key words that they remember, there may be groans from students who did not realise how hard the task is. Tell them that this first time you will give them a second reading!

3 Ask the students to work in pairs, reconstructing the sentence.

4 Bring one student to the board to act as 'secretary'. Ask the class to dictate their reconstructions to this person, who has to mediate between the different versions.

5 Finally, give the text of the sentence to one student, who reads it out slowly a couple of times so that the secretary can correct the text on the blackboard.

Acknowledgement: The first reference to 'Dictogloss' I know of came in the ELTJ in 1963, where it was described as a technique then much used in Australia. I learnt it from Jane Lockwood, an Australian, in the early 80's. In the early 90's, Ruth Wajnryb brought out a book on the 'Dictogloss' technique, *Grammar Dictation*, (Oxford 1990).

Add Words to a Dictation

Level	elementary to lower intermediate
Materials	sheets of paper / notebooks

Preparation

Select two or three paragraphs of a reading passage or dialogue from the coursebook for dictation.

1 Tell the students they are going to take the dictation down, leaving one-word spaces between each word.

2 When you have dictated a sense-group or a sentence, ask them to add one extra word somewhere in what you have just dictated.

3 At the end of the dictation, ask half a dozen people around the class to read out what they have written. This often gives you the chance to do quick, light correction of grammar points which are not clear to the students. With the speed of the dictation and the hurried additions, their grammar misunderstandings tend to come out.

Variations

a Ask students to add:
- two words
- consecutive words
- an adjective
- a colour adjective
- an adverb
- a question tag

b Ask students to take away:
- one word
- two words
- a conjunction, etc.

c You may decide to change the instructions after each sense-group or sentence.

Stripping a Passage Down

Level	elementary to advanced
Materials	photocopies of a reading passage

Preparation
Make copies of a reading passage from the last unit you have covered.

1 Give the students each a copy of the reading passage. Ask them to do the following:
- delete all the adjectives
- delete all the adverbs
- delete all the conjunctions and change the punctuation accordingly
- put a line through any subordinate clauses

2 When they have done this, the students dictate the skeletonised passage to one student at the board.

3 Pair students. Ask them to close their books and turn over their sheets and then write out the passage as it was before.

How Many Words in the Text?

Level	elementary to lower intermediate
Materials	none

1 Select a reading passage from the coursebook and ask the students to count all the words in the text. You may get asked about contractions.

2 Tell the students to go through the text and list all the words over six letters long. Check they know the meanings of the words and can pronounce them.

3 Now ask the students to make a list of all the words with two (or three) letters from the same text. Allow them to comment on what sort of words these are.

NOTE: This is a very simple language awareness exercise.

Acknowledgement: I first saw this word counting idea in the work of Michael Swan.

Matching Errors with the Correct Version

Level	elementary to advanced
Materials	80 – 100 cards for writing errors and correct versions

Preparation

Over a period of working with the coursebook, note down student errors on small cards. When you have thirty to forty incorrect utterances, write the correct versions on different cards. Shuffle the cards.

1 As the students come in to class, give each of them two or three of the shuffled cards.

2 Ask a student to read out their card. The person with the matching card reads it out. The class then votes on whose card carries the correct version. For example:

| I love my ankle | I love my uncle |
| He stole an old lady | He stole from an old lady |

If the class votes 'wrongly' you then need to tell them which the correct version is.

Variation

You could further challenge your students by getting them to grade the level of seriousness of an error.

Preparation

Collect errors from students' written work, add some perfect or near-perfect sentences and make a sheet to give out to each pair of students.

1 Pair the students and ask them to grade the gravity of the mistakes, using this scale:

1 Incomprehensible
2 Hard to understand
3 Not bad
4 Very good
5 Native speaking

2 Ask them to call out some of their gradings. Allow a general discussion to develop.

Acknowledgement: These exercises were proposed by Luke Prodromou in *IATEFL Issues*, August-September 2000.

My Favourite Mistakes

Level	elementary to advanced
Materials	none

Preparation

Tell the students about your favourite mistakes in English, either from when you were learning or nowadays. (Native speakers also make plenty of mistakes - can *you* spell /daɪəˈrɪə/?) Write your own favourite mistakes up on the board.

Ask the students to come to the next class with their half dozen favourite mistakes in English in areas like grammar, false friends, pronunciation, spelling, punctuation (who wants the semi-colon?).

1 Group the students in sixes, to share their favourite errors.

2 Each group writes the most interesting ones up on the board. Sort out any doubts the students may have.

NOTE: There are cultures in which it would be embarrassing to admit that teachers make mistakes. Only do this activity if you are comfortable with it.

Acknowledgement: I learnt this idea from Nuria Salvador, who teaches in Barcelona.

What's More English?

Level	elementary to upper intermediate
Materials	sheets of paper / notebooks

Preparation

For homework, ask students to come to the next class with twenty pattern sentences that cover some of the grammar that they have learnt in English so far. Ask them to put the sentences in three 'boxes' labelled thus:

Very English   **Neutral**   **Not Very English**

1 Explain that some students feel that certain structures and phrases are essentially English. So an Italian learner may feel that 'I am here' is very English because it is so different to 'Am here', which is what is normally said in Italian.

2 Group students in fours and ask them to compare the structures they feel to be 'very English' and those that do not feel so.

3 Bring everything together in a short whole-class feedback session. Remember your role is to draw out and listen, not to contribute your own opinions.

Grammar I Like

Level	elementary to advanced (At elementary level, the students do the activity in L1.)
Materials	sheets of paper / notebooks

1 Pair the students and ask them to go back over the last five to six units in the coursebook and pick out all the different grammar patterns they have been exposed to. Give them ten minutes.

2 Ask one student to come to the board and take dictation from the other students. They shout out the example sentences they have picked out.

3 When the board is full of example sentences, ask each student to pick out two they like and two they dislike.

4 Ask each student to come to the board and put a cross next to the two they dislike and a tick next to the two they like.

5 Choose the sentences with the most crosses and ticks and ask the students who marked them to explain why.

NOTE: When this idea of liking or disliking a grammar pattern was first published in *Grammar Games* (Rinvolucri M, Cambridge, 1984), I was amazed at the ability of students to like or dislike a particular foreign language form, but such feelings are very much there in many people.

3

Vocabulary

In coursebooks vocabulary is typically introduced in sets and carefully contextualised. However, constraints of space often mean that there isn't sufficient practice of new items that come up or opportunities for extension. Using the coursebook as a starting point, *Sets and Sequences* gives more ideas for working with vocabulary sets, and *Revising and Stretching Vocabulary* includes activities to get students to consolidate and extend what they know.

Learning the Alphabet

Level	beginner to lower intermediate (You need a class of 25 + for this activity.)
Materials	none

This is a good activity to do with primary students.

1 'Letter' each student from A to Z. If you have students left after assigning each letter of the alphabet, introduce a few more 'vowel letters' and include a couple of 'joker' students, who can represent any letter.

2 Spell out a word, for example, 'elephant', and ask the students with those letters to line up in the correct order. Then ask them each to say their letter loudly and clearly and return to their seats.

3 After several rounds with you leading, ask the student with the letter B to call out a word beginning with their letter. The students line up next to them and spell out their word. Continue with C, and so on.

Acknowledgement: I learnt this technique from a Munich secondary teacher, Irene Jakobsen.

Variation

Another way to get students to memorise the alphabet is by chanting the letters rhythmically.

1 Pair the students and demonstrate the activity with one student:

Student:	a b c d
You:	d c b a
Student:	b c d e
You:	e d c b
Student:	c d e f

Make sure that you both chant the letters rhythmically.

2 Get the pairs to work their way through the alphabet as demonstrated.

3 Circulate, helping with the pronunciation of the harder letters.

Acknowledgement: This is one of the exercises from A R Orage's *On Love and Psychological Exercises* (Samuel Weiser, 1998).

Learning Vocabulary Sequences

Level	beginner to lower intermediate
Materials	none

1 Give the students a list of the months. Drill the twelve words chorally.

2 Get half the class to say the English word chorally and the other half to say the words in L1 in response.

3 Ask for a student volunteer. In turns, ask and answer like this:

You:	January + 2?
Student:	March. July – 3?
You:	April. June – 1?
Student:	May.

4 Get the students to practise like this in pairs.

Variation

You can do this kind of vocabulary practice with vocabulary sets that are in fixed linear order, using the same question and answer technique. For example:

- Monday, Tuesday, Wednesday ...
- 1, 2, 3, 4 ...
- 6, 12, 18, 24 ...
- a, b, c, d, e, f ...

Acknowledgement: This idea comes from *Mindgame*, a vocabulary CD Rom (Fletcher de Téllez I, Clarity, Hong Kong 2000).

Number Dialogues

Level	beginner
Materials	none

If you find there is not sufficient attention given to numbers in your coursebook, this is a useful drill.

1 Get the whole class chorusing in twos up to one hundred:

'two, four, six, eight, ten ... ninety-six, ninety-eight, one hundred.'

2 Tell them to chorus in twos down from one hundred to zero.

'one hundred, ninety-eight, ninety-six, ninety-four ...'

3 Ask each student to shut their eyes and do this silently.

4 Pair the students and ask them to work backwards or forwards, as follows:

Student A: one hundred
Student B: nought
Student A: ninety-eight
Student B: two
Student A: ninety-six
Student B: four
Student A: ninety-four
Student B: six, and so on.

5 Individually, students do both sides of the above 'number dialogue' in their heads.

Reciprocal Lexical Tennis

Level	lower to upper intermediate
Materials	none

1 Choose two teams of three students. Bring them out to the front of the class, facing each other.

2 The first team 'serves' by shouting out a family word, for example, 'uncle'.

3 The other team returns the serve by shouting 'niece' or 'nephew'.

4 Award a point if a team gets one correct answer within three seconds. If they manage to get two correct answers within the time limit (i.e. niece **and** nephew), they get two points.

5 The team that has returned the serve now serves, for example, 'mother'. The other team comes back with 'child', 'son', 'daughter' or 'baby'.

6 After four or five rounds, change the teams and play until they have thoroughly explored this set of words.

Variation

Play the same game with animal males and females:

vixen / fox
bull / cow
bitch / dog

Or with reciprocal verbs like:

lend / borrow
win / lose
give / take

See *Collins COBUILD English Grammar* (Collins Cobuild, 1990) for more ideas.

Students 'Become' Words

Level	elementary to advanced
Materials	none

1 Choose one student to be 'secretary' and write up all the words recently learnt from the coursebook from a given lexical field (for example, fruit and vegetables). The secretary writes all the words the class can remember.

2 Ask the class to come up with a few more words in their mother tongue(s) which can go up on the board in English.

3 Ask the students to decide which vegetable or fruit they feel like being at the moment.

4 Tell the students to get up and mingle, explaining to different people which fruit / vegetable they are and why they chose this particular one.

Variation
Use other lexical sets. For example:

- colours
- musical instruments
- types of building
- types of land
- metals
- the main nouns and verbs used to describe a trial / courtroom.

Bilingual Word Lists Game

Level	elementary to upper intermediate
Materials	20 small pieces of card for each student

1 Ask the students to work individually and copy twenty words from the bilingual word lists in the coursebook onto small cards. Tell them to copy each word onto a separate card and put the mother tongue translations on the back of the cards.

2 Pair the students and ask them to sit facing one another.

3 Student A places a card down on the table, either way up, and student B has to shout out the translation. If student B is quick enough and gives the correct translation, they add the card to their pile. If student B is too slow in giving the answer, or gives a wrong answer, then student A takes the card back.

4 Student B now puts a card down on the table and student A has to give the translation.

The aim of the game is get all the opponent's cards.

Variation
The students can play with any number of contrasting items:

- synonyms
- opposites
- adverb / adjective pairs, for example: good / well, noisy / noisily
- adjective / verb pairs, for example: to prefer / preferable, to eat / edible
- irregular verb infinitive / simple past, for example: to teach / taught

Collective Picture

Level	elementary to upper intermediate
Materials	30 slips of paper for writing items of vocabulary, notebooks

Preparation
Select a set of concrete nouns and verbs from the last three units of the coursebook. Write about thirty of these words on slips of paper.

1 Hand out one slip of paper to each student and explain that you are going to ask the class to draw a collective picture on the board.

2 Ask each student to come up to the board and draw the word from their slip of paper. The idea is to get all the items into a coherent picture. The picture for a verb will be picture of the verb **happening**. Do the exercise without speaking. Don't intervene – let the students produce the collective picture they want.

3 Ask the class to name all the things in the picture and their parts. Get students to write the words in.

4 Individually, the students copy the drawing and the words.

5 Allow time for feedback on how building the picture felt. At low levels, let this happen in the mother tongue.

A Word's Associations

Level	elementary to upper intermediate
Materials	sheets of paper / notebooks

Preparation
Give the students a list of ten to fifteen new words to learn from the current unit in the coursebook. Ask them to think what associations they have with each word and to draw a simple picture for each one.

1 Group the students in fours and ask them to explain their pictures and the link to the word.

2 Draw half a dozen associative pictures for these words on the board, using associations of your own. Ask the students to guess what your association is in each case.

NOTE: Sharing associations allows the English words to soak into the students' minds.

Irregular Plurals in Movement

Level	beginner to advanced (depending on irregular plurals practised)
Materials	none

Preparation
Select a dozen irregular plurals that have come up in recent units.

1 Get the students to push their chairs and their desks / tables to the walls or take the students to an empty space.

2 Ask them to form two parallel lines facing you. The two columns of students should be equidistant from the side walls of the room.

3 Explain that they will be working on irregular plurals. One column is the 'singular team' and the other column is the 'plural team'.

4 If you shout out 'MOUSE', the singular team dashes across to touch their wall. The members of the plural team try to touch the members of the singular team before they reach their wall. If you shout out 'MICE', the plural team runs for their wall and the other team tries to tag (touch) them. Students who have been touched join the other team.

5 When you start playing the game, build up excitement by lingering on the initial sound to the word for several seconds, like this:

MMMMMOUSE!

NOTE: If you have a sleepy class, this activity is sure to wake them up. If you have a restless teenage class, this activity provides a release for their pent-up physical energy.

Are We Related?

Level	elementary to upper intermediate
Materials	sheets of paper / notebooks

1 In their notebooks or on a sheet of paper, ask the students to rule three columns on their page with these headings:

Correct   Sometimes Correct   Incorrect

2 Tell the students you are going to dictate sentences about family relationships. Some will be correct, some will be sometimes correct and some will be incorrect. They should write the sentences down in the appropriate column.

3 Dictate these sentences:
- My father's brother is my son.
- My name is Mary and I am my aunt's niece.
- My mother is my sister's mother. (*sometimes correct because of half-sisters*)
- My husband's father is my father-in-law.
- My brother's daughter is my niece.
- My first cousin is my father's or my mother's brother or sister's child.
- My wife's son by a previous marriage is my son-in-law.
- My great-grandfather is my dad's or my mum's grandfather.
- My wife's mother is my mother-in-law.
- My wife's brother-in-law is my brother.
- My sister's off-spring are my nephews and nieces.
- My parents' siblings are my uncles and aunts.
- My identical twin is my aunt's nephew or niece.

4 Group the students in fours, and ask them to compare their placings of the sentences.

5 Go through all the sentences with the whole class. Make sure they understand new items of vocabulary.

Acknowledgement: This exercise is an adaptation of 'Family Strips', to be found on pages 58-59, in *Teaching Adult Second Language Learners* (McKay H et al, Cambridge, 1999).

Sit Down if You Have the Word

Level	elementary to upper intermediate
Materials	none

Preparation

Go back over the last ten to fifteen units of the coursebook and pick out all the words for possessions and / or things you have. For example:

bicycle	younger sister
canoe	computer
skis	a cold

Don't collect more than thirty words.

1 Tell the class to stand up. Explain that you will shout out a word and if they have that thing or person, they should sit down.

2 After shouting out each word, get everybody back on their feet.

Variation

I have used the 'sit down' technique with all sorts of vocabulary sets:

- With adjectives that describe feelings. Students sit down when I hit on their here-and-now feeling. For example:

lonely	bored
eager	exhausted
tired	raring-to-go

- When I get to their bedtime last night:

a quarter past eight	nine o'clock
half past eight	a quarter past nine
a quarter to nine	

- When I say a food they dislike:

gnocchi	sea food
carrots	bread
spinach	rice
kimchi	

In all of these, I ask students, once they sit down, to stay seated.

Revising Vocabulary Sets

Level	elementary to upper intermediate
Materials	none

Preparation

Give the students a list of twenty to thirty words from a particular set. If the vocabulary area is 'means of transport', for example, your list might include:

tricycle	camel
fighter plane	BMW
horse	bullet train
car	suburban train
bike	ferry boat

Ask the students to study the list for homework.

1 Get the students to sit in a circle with one too few chairs for the number of students. The space inside the circle needs to be clear.

2 Tell the 'extra' student to stand in the middle of the circle and shout out, 'Anybody who has been on a jetfoil, change seats!' As some of the students move, the 'extra' student gets himself a seat, thus leaving someone else chairless. This student now leads the game.

Variation

Students can revise vocabulary from previous units by re-contextualising it like this:

If you remember where ... came, change places.

The student who becomes 'it' can then challenge any of the others who moved to prove that they really remember the context. If the person he chooses fails, that person becomes 'it', the chairless person.

Acknowledgement: I learnt this technique from Jim Wingate.

Miming Vocabulary

Level	beginner to advanced
Materials	none

Preparation
Give the students a list of thirty to forty words that have come up over the last few units and ask them to revise them for homework.

1 Ask one student to come out to the front and mime one of the words. You whisper the word in their ear. They go on miming until someone in the class shouts the word out.

2 Repeat this procedure through the thirty words with different students. Whisper into the ear of some students words that have already been mimed.

NOTE: The technique is particularly interesting at higher levels where you are dealing with abstract nouns. A student miming the word 'revocation' (as in the Revocation of the Treaty of Nantes) has a real job on their hands!

Variations on 'Simon Says'

Level	lower intermediate to advanced
Materials	none

1 Do this activity when your coursebook unit focuses on 'make' and 'do'. Explain to the students that they are to obey Simon and to disobey any direct order. For example:

You say: Simon says, 'Make your bed!'
(students mime making a bed)
You say: Simon says, 'Do your homework!'
(students mime doing homework)
You say: Make a cake!
(students stand absolutely still)

Anybody who obeys a direct order, and disobeys Simon, is out of the game.

2 Once you have completed a round of conventional 'Simon Says', tell the students they are to follow these rules:

- 'Simon says...' students obey normally
- 'O'Grady says...' students obey, doing the action as fast as they can
- 'Henk says ...' students do the opposite of what is ordered, for example, they 'unmake' the bed.
- Direct order students do absolutely nothing

Anybody who gets the rule wrong, and obeys O'Grady slowly, for example, is out of the game.

3 Allow the students to show the class what their opposites were (under 'Henk says'), getting them to name these opposites in English. Write the words up on the board.

Variation
This game is excellent for practising any group of action verbs. For example:

- stare, peek, ogle, look, glance
- run, stumble, walk, limp, jump, hop, walk backwards, tip-toe
- grin, laugh, guffaw, giggle, titter, belly laugh

It is also good for practising parts of the body:

- Touch your nose, elbow, ear, belly-button ...

Designing Words

Level	beginner to lower intermediate
Materials	sheets of paper / notebooks

1 Ask the students to work individually and retrieve twenty words that they have half forgotten from two or three units back in the coursebook. (If you are doing unit 10, ask them to go back to units 6 and 7.)

2 Pair students and ask them to 'design' the words on the page in front of them. For example, a student might write 'ladder' like this:

3 Ask the students to get up, mingle and share their designs with each other.

Acknowledgement: I learnt the designer idea from Mitch Legutke at a workshop in Hessen, Germany, in the early 80's; Morgan and I used it in *Vocabulary* (Oxford, 1986).

What it is and What it isn't

Level	lower intermediate to advanced
Materials	copies of Definition Sheet below

Preparation
In lesson 1, pair the students and give them copies of the Definition Sheet. Ask them to find out what the definitions are. For homework, ask them to write 'definition sheets' of their own for six words they think their classmates may not know, from the next six units in the coursebook.

Definition Sheet	
1	
Grammar Clue:	verb, noun
Length Clue:	three letters
Meaning Clue:	a synonym of pig
Rhyme Clue:	rhymes with 'agog'
Collocates / Combines with:	to go the whole _____ , _____wash
What is it?	_____
2	
Grammar Clue:	past participle, adjective
Length Clue:	six letters
Meaning Clue:	disappointed / stomach taken out
Rhyme Clue:	rhymes with 'jutted'
Collocates / Combines with:	absolutely _____
What is it?	_____

1 In lesson 2, group students in fours and ask them to work on their classmates' definition sheets.

2 Write all the new words on the board and check that everyone understands them.

NOTES: The answers are 1 'hog' and 2 'gutted'.

Revising what has been covered and pre-visiting the 'right hand part' of the coursebook is central to using the materials well.

Auctioning Collocations

Level	upper intermediate to advanced
Materials	copies of lists of collocations and non-collocations, hammer (optional)

Preparation

Look through the unit you have just finished, the current unit and the following unit, and pull out twelve to fifteen strong collocations. Suppose you have picked out, for example:

- essential tools
- similar techniques
- to walk down a street
- virtual world

For half the collocations chosen, create parallel non-collocations. For example:

- like techniques
- to walk down a forest

Now you have fourteen real collocations from the units and seven or eight non-collocations.

1 Assume the role of a showman. Explain that this is a 'collocations auction', and the students are going bid in pairs. There are over twenty items on sale: some are genuine and some are fakes. Each pair of auction-goers has $10,000 to bid with.

2 Pair the students. Give out copies of the list and ask the pairs to decide which phrases they want to buy.

Run the auction with all the razzmatazz you can muster, using language like:

... beautiful collocation, flows off the tongue, priceless, what am I bid for **virtual world**? Lady in blue there at the back, two hundred dollars ... two hundred and fifty! Gentleman in front here, two hundred and fifty ... Any advances on two hundred and fifty, on two hundred and fifty? Going ... going ... GONE! (hammer comes down)

3 After selling off an item, briefly tell the group whether it is genuine or fake. But be sure to sell off the fakes with as much conviction as the authentic items.

4 At the end, make sure that everybody knows which are the good collocations and which are false ones.

Variations

a You can auction a mixture of correct and incorrect sentences from the students' homework, as suggested in *Grammar Games* (Rinvolucri M, Cambridge, 1984).

b After working on a given structure, for example, the present perfect, you can auction a mixture of sentences like this:

- I am here for five days. (correct, if the reference is future)
- I am here since five days. (incorrect)
- I've been here for five days. (correct)
- I am here from five days. (incorrect)

c To teach new vocabulary, give the students a list of bilingual vocabulary with some of the translations correct and some incorrect. Here is a Spanish versus English list:

Spanish	English
mermelada	marmalade (should be 'jam')
periódico	newpaper
cuaderno	exercise book
librería	library (should be 'bookshop')

In this auction, the students only buy the correct translations.

Acknowledgement: I found auctioning being used in 1970's values clarification work and adapted it for language work. I discovered the idea in *A Practical Guide to Values Clarification* (Smith M, University Associates, La Jolla, California, 1977).

Pre-teaching Vocabulary

Level	lower intermediate to advanced
Materials	list of definitions

Preparation

Look through a reading passage in the coursebook and select twelve words that you think most of the students won't know. Prepare twelve sentences that define or contextualise each of the words. For example:

- 'BSE' is the scientific term for mad cow disease.
- Bees 'swarm' when they move from one nest to the next, they move as a black cloud or 'swarm'.

1 Dictate your defining or contextualising sentences to the students. They should only write down the words, not the rest of the sentence. Read each sentence twice.

2 Ask the students to read the passage.

3 Read the sentences a third time.

4 Ask the students to read the passage again.

Acknowledgement: I learnt this technique several years ago from Gudrun, a teacher working in Oslo.

Placing Sentences in Space

Level	lower intermediate to advanced
Materials	photocopies of reading passage, scissors for students, A3 sheets of paper

1 Tell the students to read the passage individually and ask about any difficult lexis.

2 Ask the students to cut the passage up into sentences or phrases.

3 Tell them to draw a ground plan of their house or flat on the large sheets of paper. They must use **all** the space.

4 They now place each of the cut-up sentences on the appropriate part of their ground plan. For example, a phrase like 'looking forward to hearing from you' might go by the telephone or on a desk in a study. 'We are now more vulnerable to asteroids' might go near the living room window, because it is from here you can see the sky best.

5 Group the students in fours and ask them to explain their placings.

6 Allow time for general feedback.

NOTE: For a similar exercise dealing with vocabulary, see *Vocabulary* (Morgan J et al, Oxford, 1986).

Exploring Word Meanings with Rods

Level	lower intermediate to advanced (This activity works with classes of up to 25 students.)
Materials	Cuisenaire rods

1 Take a short list of words you would like to revise from a recent unit in the coursebook. Ask the class to gather round a table so they can see the rods clearly.

2 Get four students to come and squat round the table so they do not block the others' view. Give them an abstract word like 'respect' and ask them, individually, to depict the word, using rods.

3 Ask them to explain their rod arrangements to the class. This can be done in L1.

4 Send the four students back into the group and bring out four more. Give them another word, for example, 'oppression'. They use rods to symbolise the word and explain their four arrangements to the class.

NOTE: An Arab student expressed 'respect' with a very short rod right next to a very tall rod. A Dane in the same class expressed the same words by placing two rods of nearly equal height some distance from each other. What clear cultural statements!

Acknowledgement: I learnt this use of rods from Simon Marshall, a Pilgrims colleague.

Paraphrasing Phrasal Verbs

Level	lower intermediate to advanced
Materials	copies of rewritten reading passage

Preparation
Take a reading passage from the coursebook that the students worked on two weeks ago and that presents a good number of new phrasal verbs. Rewrite the passage replacing the phrasal verbs by Latinate equivalents or semi-equivalents.

1 Hand out copies of your version of the reading passage. Ask the students to read it with their coursebooks shut. Ask them if they notice any changes.

2 Tell the students to replace all the Latinate verbs with the original phrasal verbs.

3 Ask one student to read the passage aloud to the class, with all the phrasal verbs restored.

NOTE: EFL coursebooks are odd in the way they often present the phrasal verb later than its Latinate equivalent. This order reverses the way a native-speaking child learns language: a seven-year-old will say:

'Mummy was going to the dentist tomorrow, but she put it off.'

The verb 'to postpone' would sound remote and difficult.

Acknowledgement: I learnt this technique from Christine Frank, author of *Challenge to Think* (Oxford, 1982) and *Grammar in Action Again* (Prentice Hall, 1987).

Synonyms Exercise

Level	lower intermediate to advanced
Materials	none

Preparation

Choose one of the structures being taught in the current unit and produce a long, embedded sentence including the structure. Give synonyms for the main content-words in the utterance. Suppose you are teaching delexical[1] verbs, the sentence could look like this:

They were | drinking | in the bar when she
| having a drink |

| gave an amused laugh | at someting he had
| laughed with amusement |

| made a comment | on and | gave his hand a squeeze;
| commented | | squeezed his hand;

they were | both | silent for a | while,
| each | | bit,

| taking occasional sips of their wine, | before going
| occasionally sipping their wine |

off to | have a swim.
| swim.

1 Nominate five or six students round the class to read the sentence aloud. They can choose either of the binary alternatives.

2 Rub out one of the lexical verbs, for example, 'commented on'.

3 Ask a student to read the sentence, using the delexical equivalent, 'made a comment on'.

4 Now rub out the delexical equivalent as well. The next student reads the sentence with the delexical equivalent which is no longer on the board.

5 Work your way through all the binary alternatives this way until the students are 'reading' the full sentence from a half-empty board.

NOTE: For a useful list of such verbs, see *Collins COBUILD English Grammar* (Collins Cobuild, 1990).

[1] The term 'delexical' is applied to a verb in a verb-noun combination in which the noun carries the meaning and the verb is a kind of 'empty auxiliary'. For example:
He took (delexical verb) a step towards Jack.

Synonym Reversal

Level	lower intermediate to upper intermediate
Materials	sheets of paper / notebooks

Preparation

Go through the last unit's reading passage and write in as many synonyms as you can: For example:

She walked down the | broad | avenue
| wide |

until she came to the | intersection.
| crossroads.

1 Dictate the text, with synonyms, to the class. Tell the students that their task is to take it down as it was originally.

2 Tell the students to compare their hand-written texts with the text in the book.

3 Get them to list the words and their synonyms on the board.

Vocabulary Enrichment Letters

Level	lower intermediate to advanced
Materials	Cuisenaire rods

Preparation

You will have your own personal reaction to the readings and the listening activities in the coursebook. If a particular unit annoys or interests you, write the students a letter setting out your reaction and using some of the vocabulary from the unit. In your letter, give the synonyms of some of the words you have used. Supposing your letter is about a listening on the royal family, it might look like this:

Dear | Everybody,
     | All,

     I wonder what you felt about the | passage
          | text

about the | UK | royal family. I felt it was
     | British |

a | bit | yukky. The | author | seems to think they
 | rather | | writer |

are | wonderful | people. | I don't agree. | In my
   | marvellous | | I disagree. |

view the royals are | a costly | burden to the
          | an expensive |

country. I think the Queen should | abdicate
                  | step down

and the UK should join the family of republics.

Britain has | abolished | the old Lords,
       | done away with |

so why not the monarchy?

1 Give each student a copy of your letter and ask them to choose which of each word pair they prefer.

2 Ask a student to come to the board and write up all the word pairs.

3 Ask all the students to come out and tick each of the words they like better than its synonym.

4 Ask round the class about particular preferences.

5 As homework, each student replies to your letter.

4

Reading

The reading texts in your coursebook are often an underused resource. *New Ways with Reading Texts* offers suggestions of how you can return to the texts to exploit them better. *Comprehension and Summarising* includes alternative activities to reinforce those in the coursebook.

Rub-outs

Level	elementary to upper intermediate
Materials	none

Preparation
Write up a couple of paragraphs of a text from the coursebook on the board. This is best done with a text that has a good rhythm, like a song text, a poem or a rhyme, but you can do it with any text.

1 Ask a student to read the whole text through. Ask for a second reading by someone else.

2 Erase half a dozen words in different places in the text. Ask the next student to read the text, including the missing words.

3 Delete three or four more words and ask for another reading that still includes all the words.

4 Continue this process until the class can read the whole piece from a blank board.

NOTE: This is a very old memorising activity that has really stood the test of time well. Some students love learning texts by rote.

Look, No Spaces!

Level	elementary to upper intermediate
Materials	re-keyed text on disk

Preparation
Re-key one or two paragraphs of the coursebook text you want the students to work on, deletingallthespaces betweenwords. Put your text onto a floppy disk and book the computer room.

1 Send your 'merged' text out to the students' computers and get them working two to a machine.

2 Tell them to space the text correctly.

3 Get the students to compare their version with the text in the coursebook.

Variation
Give the students the merged text in a hand-out and get them to insert slashes at the word boundaries.

Acknowledgement: Marjorie Baudains learnt the merging idea from early Latin text and I learnt it from her book, *Alternatives* (Pilgrims-Longman, 1990).

Cyclical Repetition

Level	beginner to lower intermediate
Materials	none

1 Once the students have understood and practised a rhyme or short poem from the coursebook, tell them to work individually and rewrite one line of it several times so that the word deleted from the **left** of the sentence goes to the **right**. For example:

Jack and Jill went up the hill
    and Jill went up the hill Jack

Ask them to line up the text in columns, like this:

Jack	and	Jill	went	up	the	hill
and	Jill	went	up	the	hill	Jack
Jill	went	up	the	hill	Jack	and
went	up	the	hill	Jack	and	Jill
up	the	hill	Jack	and	Jill	went
the	hill	Jack	and	Jill	went	up
hill	Jack	and	Jill	went	up	the
Jack	and	Jill	went	up	the	hill

2 Ask a couple of students to read the left hand vertical column of words and the right hand column aloud to the class.

3 Pair the students and ask them to take turns reading the new poem to each other with as much meaning as possible.

Acknowledgement: This activity comes from *On Love and Psychological Exercises* (Orage A R, Samuel Weiser, 1998).

Translation into Sign Language

Level	elementary to upper intermediate
Materials	none

Preparation
Choose a poem, a song or some passage with a strong meaning from your coursebook. Select about eight lines to work on.

1 Make sure that everybody knows what 'sign language' is and ask the students to show each other a few signs in the sign language corresponding to their L1 if they know them.

2 Group students in threes and ask them to translate the short passage you have selected into their personal approximation of sign language. They can invent freely.

3 Invite some of the threesomes to 'sign' the passage, then allow some time for feedback on the activity.

NOTE: In this lesson the most fidgety, kinaesthetic students come into their own.

Acknowledgement: I learnt the idea of translating a text into a variant of sign language from Peter Grundy and Susan Bassnett's *Language through Literature* (Pilgrims-Longman, 1993).

Text All Over the Place

Level	elementary to lower intermediate
Materials	enlarged copies of dialogue, notebooks

Preparation

Choose a dialogue from the coursebook and make three enlarged photocopies. The letters need to be huge.

Cut each of the enlarged copies into ten to fifteen sections and place these all over the classroom: on the ceiling, under the desks, on the back of chairs, on your own back and on the floor and walls.

1 Get the students go round the room and transcribe the whole of the dialogue into their notebooks, re-establishing the correct order.

2 Tell the students to compare their transcriptions with the dialogue in the coursebook.

NOTE: Is your class too unruly? Don't you dare to try this with them? If they are unruly, maybe it is because they hate sitting still. This exercise gets them moving.

Acknowledgement: I learnt this idea from a Northumberland secondary school teacher of French.

Turn Text into an Art Gallery

Level	lower intermediate to advanced
Materials	copy of text, sheets of paper

Preparation

Choose a narrative text from the coursebook and make a copy of it. Select about twelve two- or three-line snippets and cut them out. Put these up round the walls of the classroom in the correct sequence before the lesson starts.

1 Explain to the students that today their room is an art gallery. The pieces of text up round the walls are the captions under twelve large pictures.

2 Tell the students to walk round, read the captions and imagine the pictures in their mind's eye.

3 Get each student to draw the picture that most interests them, using colour if possible.

4 Invite some students to describe their pictures to the whole class.

5 Tell the class to read the original text in the coursebook.

Acknowledgement: Silvia Stephan from South Germany showed this technique to Pilgrims colleagues in the summer of 2000.

Snippets from Reading Passages

Level	elementary to upper intermediate
Materials	none

Preparation

When you are getting towards the end of your coursebook, give each student in the class one reading passage from a previous unit to revise very thoroughly for homework. Ask each student to come ready to reproduce the passage in their own words. Suggest that a good way is to mumble the text to themselves in English.

1 Ask the students to shut their eyes and mumble their text through to themselves without reference to the book.

2 Tell the students they are going to mumble their text again but that at a certain moment you will ask one student to continue the text aloud. At this moment all the others hold their text at the point they have got to and listen.

3 Only allow the first student to say two or three sentences, before you quickly nominate a second student, who carries on their text from where the last student stopped. Go round a dozen students this way, inviting them to give snippets of their text.

4 The students go back to mumbling their text for twenty seconds and then you have another round of snippets.

5 Tell them to go to the person whose whole text they feel like listening to.

NOTE: Mumbling is an important technique to introduce to language learners. It is a technique used naturally by some of the best language learners.

Acknowledgement: I learnt this activity from Anne Pechou from Toulouse. She used it with the students' own freely-selected stories.

Miming the Reading Passage

Level	beginner to advanced
Materials	none

Preparation

Ask three or four students to prepare to mime a dozen small sections from the next reading passage in the coursebook. They read the passage and decide which parts they can convincingly mime. They do this for homework.

1 Ask the whole class to read the passage and check they know all the words.

2 Tell the class the first student is going to do twelve very short mimes. After seeing each mime, the students underline the words in the text they think inspired the mime.

3 After the first twelve mimes, get the students to shout out the items of language they have underlined.

4 Repeat the procedure with the other three miming students.

Behead the Words

Level	elementary to lower intermediate
Materials	copies of 'beheaded' text

Preparation

Select a reading passage from the coursebook and re-key it _eaving _ut _ll _he _nitial _etters, but leaving space for their inclusion by the students.

1 Pair the students and ask them to close their coursebooks.

2 Give out copies of your 'beheaded' text and ask them to put in the missing letters.

3 Tell the students to compare their text with the original in the coursebook.

NOTES: This is a good exercise to do in the computer room.

In her book *Lessons from the Learner* (Pilgrims-Longman 1990), Sheelagh Deller tells us to get all 'busy work' done by students. So, instead of decapitating the text yourself, why not get students from a higher level class to do it for you? They will learn a lot about word shape and spelling as they delete the initial letters.

Students Correct Semantic Errors

Level	elementary to advanced
Materials	copies of prepared text with errors

Preparation

Take three paragraphs of the coursebook text and rewrite them with a dozen semantic errors. Copy the rewritten paragraphs so you can give out one to each student.

1 Give out the copies of your text and ask the students to correct them, keeping their coursebooks closed.

2 Check for any items they could not correct or did not understand.

3 Pair the students and ask them to go back to a previous unit. Leave it up to each pair which passage they choose. Ask them to rewrite two paragraphs, messing up the text semantically and humorously.

4 Get the pairs to exchange their messed-up texts with other pairs, who then correct them.

5 Ask the students which they liked best, correcting messed-up text, or messing up the text for someone else to correct.

NOTE: Despite its appearance of burlesque, this is a very searching close reading and editing exercise.

Variation

With a monolingual class, you can use translation errors.

Preparation

Take two paragraphs from a reading passage in the coursebook and translate them into the students' mother tongue. Introduce between seven and nine translation errors, grammatical and lexical.

1 Group the students in threes, give them your translation and ask them if they can spot the deliberate errors.

2 Do a whole-class round-up of the activity.

Text Reading Duet

Level	beginner to lower intermediate
Materials	sheets of paper

Preparation
In lesson 1, select a text from the coursebook. Pair the students and tell them to copy out half the text each. They should write on separate sheets of paper.

- In a poem or a song, student A copies the first line, student B the second, student A the third, etc.
- In a dialogue, student A copies the first utterance and student B the second, student A the third, etc.
- In a prose text, the students copy out alternate sentences.

For homework, each student learns their half of the text by heart.

1 In lesson 2, tell the students to put their coursebooks away and get the pairs to work simultaneously, producing the text as a duet, each speaking their part.

2 Bring the class together and ask the pairs to perform their duet in a variety of ways:

- whispering it
- saying it sadly
- saying it as deep as they can
- saying it as squeakily as they can
- saying it as though they were very old people
- saying it with as foreign an accent as they can
- saying it with as English an accent as they can
- saying it as if they were six-year-olds
- saying it like a robot
- saying it in the voice of a well-known TV announcer

NOTE: Rote learning is brilliant language practice for some students. They really get satisfaction from it. These tend to be the auditorily-gifted people and often good language learners. It has always been central in some learning traditions, while you rarely see it proposed in current UK- or US-produced EFL books.

Acknowledgement: This unit lies within the de la Garanderie Number 2 Way of Learning. For more on this, see: *Ways of Doing* (Davis et al, Cambridge, 1999), pages 122-124.

You Read, They Complete or Correct

Level	elementary to lower intermediate
Materials	none

1 Once the students have dealt with some of the difficulties in the reading text in the current unit, tell them you are going to read the passage to them, stopping every now and then for them to finish the phrase.

2 Tell the students to close their coursebooks. Read the passage to them three times, stopping at different points. Where you stop is where their attention will focus, so you can get them thinking about grammar, link words, collocations, depending on your aims in this lesson.

Variation
Tell the students you are going to read the text to them continuously, but this time with some words wrong. They should interrupt immediately and correct you. For example, if the text says 'she grabs his arm' you mis-read 'she grabs his leg', etc. Teenage students love this.

Acknowledgement: I learnt this idea from Robert O'Neill in 1971, when his book *Kernel Lessons Intermediate* (Longman, 1971), fell from heaven into my hands. It was a Godsend.

Cross the Questions Out

Level	elementary to upper intermediate
Materials	copies of list of questions

Preparation

Prepare a very large number of questions about a reading passage from the coursebook. For a normal length intermediate passage, you might want to write between forty and fifty questions. For example, if this is the passage,

Father: What time did you come home last night, then, Mary?

Mary: Oh, not sure, 'bout half one, I think.

Father: Half past one? I didn't hear you.

Mary: Came in quietly. I didn't want to wake you up.

then these could be the questions:

- What time did Mary say she came in?
- How old is Mary?
- Where are they talking?
- What time is it when they talk?
- How old is the father?
- What does Mary's hair look like?
- Is the father deaf?
- What is Mary wearing?
- Think of someone you know. Who would they sympathise with in this dialogue?
- How, exactly, did Mary come in quietly?
- What is the weather like as they talk?
- What is Mary's mood?
- Does the dialogue remind you of things you have experienced?

1 Ask the students to read the passage and then give them your long list of questions.

2 Tell them to read through the questions and cross out all the ones they do not like.

3 Pair the students. Within the pairs, A and B exchange question pages. Student A then asks student B the questions they have not crossed out, and student B answers them.

4 Get the pairs to do it the other way round.

Variation

After the 'crossing the questions out' phase, the pairs do not exchange papers. Instead, they put their own retained questions to their partners.

NOTES: This is a double reading comprehension lesson, as thinking through the long list of questions and deciding which to eliminate is real editorial reading.

For another example of this technique in action, see 'Revenge Questions' in *Once Upon a Time* (Morgan J et al, Cambridge, 1983).

Students Write Comprehension Questions

Level	elementary to advanced
Materials	sheets of paper

1 Ask the students to read a passage you have selected from the coursebook.

2 Group the students in fours. Tell each group to prepare seven comprehension questions in writing for the next group.

3 Ask the groups to exchange comprehension questions and to work in eights, answering the fourteen questions.

4 Round off with a whole-class session in which questions no one could answer in the groups of eight are put to the whole class.

Acknowledgement: I learnt this technique from Marjorie and Richard Baudains, who published it in *Alternatives* (Pilgrims-Longman, 1990).

Variation

You could do a similar activity, but allow students to choose who should answer the questions individually.

1 Ask the students to read a passage you have selected from the coursebook.

2 Ask each one to write between seven and ten questions about the passage and to address each question to another named person in the class. The questions can be about language difficulties, ideas in the passage, another person's opinion, etc.

3 Get the students up and moving around. They have to put their questions to the named addressees.

NOTE: You could join in the questioning or you could walk around, observing. This exercise gives you a chance to learn a great deal about your students.

Dialogue on the Board

Level	lower intermediate to advanced
Materials	sheets of paper / notebooks

1 Ask the students to read carefully through a passage you have selected from the coursebook carefully.

2 Divide the board space up into two areas. If you have limited board space, bring in large sheets that you can put up on the wall at the front of the class.

Questions	Comments

3 Tell the students to come and write up any questions they want the class (or you) to answer.

4 Ask them to write up any comments they want to make on the reading passage. There should be a space after each question or comment for an answer or a counter-comment.

5 Allow the students to conduct this board dialogue in silence for about ten minutes, then let the silence give way to a whole-class discussion.

Acknowledgement: I learnt this technique twenty years ago from an Austrian colleague on a Pilgrims course.

Bartering Opinions

Level	lower intermediate to advanced
Materials	slips of paper for writing comments

1 Ask the students to read the text in the unit carefully and then get them to write down five or six comments on the text, or questions about the text, each on a separate slip of paper. They could be about the language in the text, about the intellectual and emotional content of the text, or about other things roused in the student by the text itself.

2 Tell the students to get up, move around the room and barter their slips of paper. For example, Tomoko goes up to Jaroslav and shows him her comments and questions. Suppose he wants the third one, she will only give it to him if he has a question or comment she wants to have. If he hasn't, they break off negotiations; if he has, they exchange.

The students' aim is to get rid of all the slips of paper that are in their own handwriting.

Acknowledgement: I first learnt this technique from Marjorie and Richard Baudains, authors of *Alternatives* (Pilgrims-Longman, 1990).

Involvement Reading

Level	lower intermediate to advanced
Materials	none

Preparation
Read through the next unit's reading passage, thinking of all it contains in terms of:

- grammar
- style
- rich vocabulary
- culture
- things that are personally meaningful to you

1 Tell the students to read the first paragraph. Check that they know all the words and then give your various comments, according to the language knowledge and age of the students.

2 Ask one of the students to read the next section and give their comments.

3 Read the next part yourself and comment.

4 Ask another student to read and comment, and so on.

Acknowledgement: This simple, natural way of dealing with a text was demonstrated by Theresa Zanatta in a workshop in a Language Teacher's conference in Beirut, May 2000.

Summarising the Text

Level	lower intermediate to advanced
Materials	notebooks

1 Select a fairly long reading passage from the coursebook.

2 Divide the class up into four equal-sized groups, but ask the students to work on their own.

3 Ask the students to read a text with these tasks in mind:
- **Group 1:** Pick out 8-12 key words or phrases from the text.
- **Group 2:** Summarise the main content of the passage in one sentence.
- **Group 3:** Summarise the main content in one paragraph (maximum four sentences).
- **Group 4:** Notice their own reaction to the text and express this in 5-10 key words.

4 Group the students in fours, with one person from each of the above groups.

5 Tell the students to share the work they have been doing.

6 Leave time for a short, whole-class feedback on how they experienced the different tasks.

Reading Without Reading

Level	lower intermediate to advanced
Materials	sheets of paper / notebooks

1 Select a fairly long passage from the coursebook and ask the students to underline the first and last sentences in each paragraph.

2 Tell the students to close the coursebook and make notes of what they have understood from the underlined sentences.

3 Group the students in fours to discuss their notes, without referring to the text.

4 Give the class five to ten things to scan the text for.

5 Ask the groups to work together again and discuss what they found, with the coursebooks closed.

6 Pair the students and tell them to summarise the text in a given number of words.

7 Put the summaries on the walls so that the students can move around and read each others' work, then tell everybody to read the text.

Acknowledgement: I learnt this technique from a Portuguese colleague at Pilgrims in July 1994. Her name was Elisabeta.

Sets of Three Words

Level	lower intermediate to advanced
Materials	slips of paper for writing words

Preparation

Select a reading passage from the coursebook and pull out between twenty-one and twenty-four key words.

1 Write up the key words on the board, but not in the order they come in the text.

2 Group the students in threes and ask them to write down the words, each on a different slip of paper.

3 Tell the groups that they need to put the words in sense-groups of three. They should end up with **seven** groups of **three** words.

4 Get the students to mingle and look at the way other threesomes have done the task.

5 Tell the students to read the passage silently.

NOTE: As they classify the words, they are preparing a mapping of the text they are drawn from

Acknowledgement: This idea comes from *Vocabulary* (Morgan J et al, Oxford, 1986).

I Understand Three Things

Level	elementary to upper intermediate
Materials	sheets of paper / notebooks

1 Choose a very hard reading passage from the coursebook (one several units ahead). Ask the students to scan through the passage on their own.

2 Ask them to scan through a second time and simply write down **three things** they have understood. These can be tiny details or three sentences that summarise the main gist of the text. Each student can work at his or her own comprehension level.

3 Bring the students together in groups of four to compare their sentences.

NOTE: It is useful to jump forward in the coursebook so that students can get to know the ground ahead of them. This is as important as going back to old units to re-map the terrain already covered.

Acknowledgement: Rainer Pirkner, a Munich secondary school teacher, uses this technique with difficult technical texts from the Internet.

5

Writing

The coursebook provides the writing model, but it is often hard to get your students to branch out or check what they have written. With this in mind, *Think Big, Think Small* provides activities to encourage students to write a fuller text themselves as well as activities looking at the smaller details of the text. *Writing Freely* suggests ways to encourage more personalised writing.

Expanding a Skeletal Dialogue

Level	elementary to lower intermediate
Materials	copies of skeletal dialogue

Preparation

Choose a dialogue from your coursebook and reduce each utterance to two-word 'sentences'. It could look like this:

A: More coffee?
B: No, thanks.
A: Anything else?
B: Bill, please.
A: Right away.
B: Service included?
A: Actually, no.

1 Pair the students. Give each pair a copy of the skeletal dialogue and ask them to expand it to a more normal length, making it less telegraphic. They might expand the example to:

A: Would you like some more coffee?
B: No, thanks. I've had enough.
A: Would you like anything else?

2 Ask several pairs to read out their expanded dialogues.

3 Tell the students to read the original coursebook dialogue.

Acknowledgement: This idea comes from Emma Walton, TTI School of English, Camden Town, London.

The Opposite of the Text

Level	elementary to lower intermediate
Materials	none

1 Choose a part of the next unit's reading passage to dictate.

2 Pair the students. Tell one student in each pair to take down the dictation as you say it. The other student should wait until a full sentence has been dictated and then rewrite the sentence as its opposite. For example, a sentence dictated as 'she went up' might become 'he went down' or 'he stayed down'. How sophisticated the reversal is will depend on the group and the level.

Allow time after each sentence for the paired partners to consult each other.

3 After the dictation, give the students time to check and correct the new passage they have written. They may need to change things to make the text coherent.

4 Invite some of the pairs to read their new texts out.

The Optimist and the Pessimist

Level	lower to upper intermediate
Materials	sheets of paper

1 Ask each student to fold and tear a piece of paper into seven strips.

2 Pair the students and tell them one is to choose the role of the Optimist and the other the role of the Pessimist.

3 Dictate a first line to all the pairs. For example:
This woman's dog likes eating chocolate.

4 Simultaneously, the Optimist in each pair writes a reaction on their first slip of paper starting with 'Fortunately ...', while the Pessimist writes a reaction starting with 'Unfortunately ...'

5 Tell the Optimists to place their sentences after the initial statement. The Pessimists then place their sentences in third position.

6 Tell the Optimists and Pessimists to simultaneously write reactions to the third sentence, each starting with their respective adverb. The Pessimists place their sentences in fourth position, while the Optimists place theirs in fifth place.

7 Tell them to react to the fifth sentence, and so on, until their seven slips are all used up.

8 When the writing phase is over, invite two or three pairs to read out their surreal dialogues to the class.

Editing Down

Level	elementary to advanced
Materials	copies of a reading text from the coursebook, sheets of paper

1 Hand out copies of the reading text. Tell students that you want them to strip out any words they feel are not essential from the first three paragraphs. Give them an example, taking out adjectives, adverbs, and so on.

2 Ask the students to work individually. Tell them to cross out the superfluous words, making them illegible. They should write these words out on a separate sheet of paper.

3 Pair the students. Ask them to exchange copies of the texts and try to replace the words that their partners have crossed out.

4 Tell the students to exchange their sheets of paper with the missing words and check.

Student-generated Cloze Text

Level	elementary to upper intermediate
Materials	sheets of paper, notebooks

Preparation

In lesson 1, ask the students to choose a reading passage several units ahead in the coursebook. They should read through it and use their dictionary to deal with unknown words. Tell them to rewrite the passage, leaving out between ten and fifteen consecutive pairs of words. They need to make sure they leave good spaces where the words have been left out.

1 In lesson 2, ask the students to exchange papers with a student sitting the other side of the room from them. The coursebook should be firmly shut.

2 Ask the students to do the cloze exercise.

3 Once they have finished, tell the students to move over to sit with their partner and check through their texts.

NOTE: To avoid the step-by-step boredom of coursebook teaching it is good to range both back and forward across the units. Hence the suggestion of using this cloze technique on a unit way ahead in the book.

Acknowledgement: Why should teachers waste precious time producing gap-fill material, when having the students create the exercise actually teaches them something? For more exercises like this, see Sheelagh Deller's *Lessons from the Learner* (Pilgrims-Longman, 1990).

Punctuation Matters

Level	elementary to upper intermediate
Materials	re-keyed text

Preparation

Take a dialogue from the coursebook and re-key it as if it were continuous text, omitting all punctuation.

1 Pair the students and ask them to rewrite the text as a normal dialogue, reinstating the punctuation.

2 Tell the students to open the coursebook and compare their edit with the original text.

NOTE: For auditorily-aware students, work on punctuation focuses on rhythm and intonation.

Variation

You could also put your re-keyed text onto a floppy disk and book the computer room. Send your 'merged' text out to the students' computers and get them working two to a machine.

Vertical Dialogues

Level	beginner to lower intermediate
Materials	none

1 Choose a short dialogue from the coursebook and start to rewrite it vertically on the board. See below.

2 Ask the students to continue rewriting the dialogue vertically. They should rewrite it in vertical lines, starting from the outside left and the outside right. Remind them to leave enough space in the middle to fit the whole dialogue in. For example:

A1	A2		B2	B1
H	N		G	Y
i	o		l	o
!	t		a	u
			d	
	t			O
	o		t	K
	o		o	?
	b		h	
	a		e	
	d		a	
	.		r	
			i	
			t	
			.	

3 Pair the students and ask them to read the dialogue.

NOTE: This exercise helps students to perceive a dialogue visually as well as to focus on spelling in a new way.

Writing Dialogues Backwards

Level	beginner to lower intermediate
Materials	sheets of paper / notebooks

1 Write the beginning of a dialogue up on the board like this:

A: You haven't done your homework.

.lli saw I tub ,yrroS **:B**

A: You made the same excuse last week!

.skeew eerht rof kcis neeb ev'I **:B**

2 Ask the students to copy out the dialogue you want them to work on in their coursebook in this forward-backwards way.

3 Pair the students and tell them to read the dialogue until they get fluent in both roles.

NOTE: This exercise brings the talents of dyslexic students to the fore. They have great flexibility in reading direction.

Acknowledgement: Both of these ideas came up in a workshop Jim Wingate led at Pilgrims in the summer of 2000.

Letters Addressed to Objects

Level	lower intermediate to advanced
Materials	sheets of paper

1 Ask each student to think for a moment and decide what object or other character they would like to be right now, if they could temporarily escape from being themselves. Give them an example of who or what **you** might want to become:

I would like to become a middle-sized rock on a Himalayan hillside.
or
I want to be the US president's guardian angel.
or
I am a tabby cat curled up by the fireside.

2 Pair the students. Get student A to ask student B what role student B has chosen and then ask a few questions to help develop that role. Allow four minutes for this.

3 Ask the pairs to swap over, so that now student B asks student A questions to help student A develop the role they have chosen. Allow four more minutes.

4 Tell the students to work on their own and write a letter from their real self to their role self. Tell them to write a page and give them a fifteen-minute time limit.

5 They should now 'role-reverse', that is, become the role being or object and answer the letter they have just received. Allow fifteen minutes again.

6 Tell the original pairs to get together in groups of six and read out the two letters they have written in their groups.

7 Allow a few minutes for whole-class feedback.

Variation

1 Do steps 1 to 3 suggested above and then group the students in eights.

2 Ask each student to introduce their partner to the group.

3 Now explain that each person can write a letter to the role or object of their choice within their group.

4 Get the students to write from their real selves to the roles.

5 On receiving a letter, the students should reply in role, but writing to the real person.

Acknowledgement: For a fuller explanation of this variation and for a wealth of other imaginative writing exercises, see *Letters* (Burbidge et al, Oxford, 1996).

Writing from a Group Picture

Level	elementary to upper intermediate
Materials	sheets of paper / notebooks

1 Tell the students they are going to produce a group picture. Each student can come up and draw one thing on the board. A student may come to the board more than once, but each time they can only draw one element.

2 Sit at the back of the class and watch the picture take shape. This can be magic, as the group expresses itself non-linguistically.

3 Ask each student to work on their own and write a dialogue between any two objects / beings in the picture. They choose their objects / people silently and individually.

4 Group the students in fours and ask them to read out their dialogues to each other.

5 Three or four students can be invited to read their dialogues to the whole class.

My View of Three

Level	elementary to upper intermediate
Materials	sheets of paper

1 Ask each student to draw the figure 3 in the middle of a clean sheet of paper.

2 Tell the students to write five sentences in the form of a rose out from the figure in the middle of the page. They should write sentences about the ideas they have about the figure 3. My students have written things like this:

3 Group the students in fours to compare sentences.

4 Ask each group to write their three most interesting sentences on the board.

Who Wrote This Coursebook?

Level	elementary to advanced
Materials	sheets of paper

Preparation
When your students have done between eight and ten units of the book, ask them, for homework, to write short profiles of what sort of people they imagine the coursebook author/s to be.

1 Ask the students to put their profiles up round the walls of the classroom and go round reading the other profiles.

2 With the help of a student 'secretary' at the board, ask them to write a polite collective letter to the author/s, asking to be sent a real profile or profiles of the writer/s. The letters should also explain that their imagined profiles are enclosed for the author's / authors' enjoyment.

3 Send the letter to the author/s, care of the publisher.

NOTE: Writing a letter to real English speakers outside the learning group focuses the students' minds on accuracy. They do not want to write unacceptable English.

Which Was the Most Boring?

Level	beginner to advanced
Materials	none

Preparation
As homework, ask the students to go back over the past ten units and decide which was:

● the most **boring** unit
● the most **interesting** unit
● the most **unexpected** unit

and why.

1 Ask the students to write a paragraph about the most **boring** unit.

2 Ask a few of them read out their paragraphs.

3 In fours, get the students to share their feelings about the units.

4 Invite general feedback from the whole group and then give your own feelings and reasons.

NOTE: This activity is especially useful with teenagers. It accepts the reality of student feelings and suggests you get them to share these feelings.

6

Listening

However carefully designed, the coursebook listenings are often treated with considerable trepidation by the students. Referring closely to the coursebook, this section includes a range of activities specifically aimed at overcoming anxiety. It starts off with alternative ways of treating dictations (including getting the students up and moving around the class). *A Personal Response* includes activities that draw on the things that students hear and think about apart from the words in the text. Finally, *Listening Comprehension without Fear* suggests ideas for making students' listening 'anxiety-free'.

Banana Dictation

Level	elementary to lower intermediate
Materials	cassette / CD player, sheets of paper / notebooks

Preparation
Decide which grammar or vocabulary you want the students to concentrate on in the next listening passage in the coursebook. Prepare a dictation omitting the key words you would like them to focus on.

1 Tell the students you are going to dictate a text to them in which they will frequently hear the word 'banana'. Tell them to leave a large gap every time they hear 'banana'. For example:

I live BANANA London, only five minutes' walk BANANA the river.

2 Dictate the listening passage, saying 'banana' in place of the words you want them to focus on.

3 Pair the students and ask them to work out what might fit in the blanks.

4 Play the listening so the students can check how well they filled the blanks in.

Acknowledgement: I learnt about 'banana dictations' from Paul Rogerson's article in *Europa Vicina*, No 6, March 2000, the AISLI magazine, Italy.

From Dictated Snippets to Full Listening

Level	elementary to lower intermediate
Materials	cassette / CD player, sheets of paper / notebooks

Preparation
Go through the transcript of the listening text in the next unit and underline five to seven sentences that seem to carry the gist.

1 Tell the students that you are a 'dictation machine'. To make you work, they have to shout out one of these three commands:

Start!
Stop!
Go back to ...

2 Tell them that the text you will dictate to them consists of selected sentences from a text they will listen to later.

3 The students get you to 'Start!'. You go on reading till someone shouts 'Stop!'. You 'stop', 'start' and 'go back to...' with total accuracy. If the students stop you mid-word, you stop right there. When they say 'Start!', you start from exactly that point.

4 After the dictation, play them the whole listening twice.

Acknowledgement: I learnt this technique from Tessa Woodward in *The Recipe Book* (ed. Lindstromberg, Pilgrims-Longman, 1993).

Listen, Run and Write

Level	elementary to lower intermediate
Materials	small, portable cassette / CD player, copies of dialogue, sheets of paper / notebooks

Preparation
Pick a short dialogue from the coursebook and photocopy the transcript.

1 Group the students in threes. Ask one student from each group to come outside with you. Take the cassette player with you. The other two should sit with pen and paper at the ready.

2 Tell the students who you take outside that you will play the dialogue several times. Their job is to remember it line by line, run back into the classroom and dictate to their partners as fast as they can. Offer a prize for the first finishers. Play the cassette softly to avoid complaints from colleagues!

3 When the runners have been backwards and forwards half a dozen times, they exchange roles with one of the two 'writers' in their group, so that each person gets a turn at listening and running.

4 Give the students the transcripts so they can correct their dictations.

Read, Say, Hear, Say, Write

Level	elementary to intermediate
Materials	copies of a text, sheets of paper / notebooks

Preparation
Choose two or three paragraphs from a passage in the coursebook. You can usefully use this technique with a poem. Make several copies. Put these up outside your classroom, a little way down the corridor.

1 Group the students in threes. Tell the members of the groups to do as follows:
- Student A to go outside into the corridor.
- Student B to stand at the door of the classroom.
- Student C to be in the classroom, as far from the door as possible.

2 Their tasks are as follows:
- Student A reads a small part of the text on the wall and brings it back **as far as the classroom door** and says it to student B.
- Student B then goes across the room and dictates it to C.
- Student C writes down what student B says.

3 Halfway through the exercise, tell the students in each team to exchange roles.

4 When the teams have finished, tell them to open their coursebooks and check what they have written.

Acknowledgement: 'Running dictation' appeared in book form in Davis' book, *Dictation* (Cambridge, 1989). In the original activity students worked in pairs, not threes. There was a reader-runner and a writer. This 'threesome' version is richer in terms of the language skills being used.

Gap Dictation

Level	elementary to upper intermediate
Materials	cassette / CD player, copies of listening with words whited out, sheets of paper / notebooks

Preparation
Take the transcript of a listening text from the coursebook and 'white out' one third of the sentences or sense-groups. Make a photocopy for each student.

1 Play the listening through once.

2 Give the students the transcript with the blanks. As they listen again, ask them to fill them in mentally.

3 Explain that you are going to dictate the missing parts, but not in order. The students should write the sentences down on another piece of paper, not on the transcript. Ask one student to write their dictated missing parts on the board.

4 After dictating each sentence or sense group, ask the board writer if they have any doubts about what they have just written. If there are problems they can't see, underline the faulty items and get someone from the class to come out and correct them.

5 After the dictation, pair the students and ask them to copy their correct sentences into the transcript blanks.

6 Play the whole listening through again.

Acknowledgement: Jane Hoelker, of Seoul National University, proposed this technique in *The Language Teacher*, March 2000. She writes, 'I first learnt this activity fifteen years ago in a newsletter I picked up in a faculty room.' This is typical of how ELT methodology is transmitted.

Four Voice Dictation

Level	elementary to upper intermediate
Materials	copy of text, sheets of paper / notebooks

Preparation
Make one copy of a coursebook text and then divide it into four roughly equal parts.

1 Organise the students so that they are sitting in four blocks in the classroom with their coursebooks shut.

2 Ask for a volunteer from each block. Give each volunteer one quarter of the passage and tell them to dictate their part of the text to their group. Each 'dictator' should stand as far from his group as the room allows. (This is a noisy exercise and you may want to warn colleagues with classrooms either side of yours.)

3 Tell the students who have been writing to open their coursebooks and check their spelling. The first time you use a quadrophonic dictation, allow a few moments for feedback.

Acknowledgement: I learnt this exercise from Herbert Puchta, author of *Creative Grammar Practice* (Pilgrims-Longman, 1993).

Capitalising Stress

Level	beginner to lower intermediate
Materials	sheets of paper / notebooks

1 Dictate two paragraphs from a reading passage from a previous unit and ask the students to write the stressed syllables in capital letters. Give them an example on the board:

Good MORNing, CONnie.

2 After the dictation, ask one student to dictate the paragraphs back to you. Write them on the board so everyone can check spelling and capitalisation.

3 Pair the students and ask them to read the paragraphs to each other, exaggerating the stress.

Acknowledgement: Paul Seligson demonstrated this technique at the APAC Conference, in Barcelona, March 2001.

Dictation with Mother-tongue Accent

Level	elementary to lower intermediate
Materials	cassette / CD player, notebooks / sheets of paper

1 Select a listening passage from the current unit of the coursebook. Dictate the first sentence in a heavy mother-tongue accent (if you have a multi-lingual class, dictate in the accent of the largest language grouping).

2 Once the students have written the sentence down, ask them what they noticed about the way you spoke. Tell them you will repeat the sentence with the same accent and they are to correct you, 'Not mmmmm, teacher, you should say pppppppppp.'

3 Dictate the second sentence in the same accent and ask them to correct you and write at the same time. Continue this way to the end of the text you have chosen.

4 Play them the passage from the cassette.

5 Ask half the class to read the passage chorally in as English a way as possible while the other half of the class reads it with as heavy an accent as possible.

6 Get the two halves of the class swap roles.

NOTE: This is a fun exercise in contrastive phonology. Students love mock-correcting their teacher, especially teenagers. An exaggerated foreign accent draws sharp attention to the way English should be pronounced, so a Spanish 'jai jam a bery unjappy estoodent' sets off the correct form: 'I am a very unhappy student'.

Pictures in my Listening

Level	beginner to lower intermediate
Materials	cassette / CD player

1 Ask the students to shut their eyes and to become aware of how they are breathing but not change it.

2 Ask them to open their eyes and listen to the text once, just letting the words flow over them.

3 Tell the students they will now have three more listenings. They are to notice the pictures that come into their minds as they listen and jot down either a simple sketch, a word in their mother tongue or a word in English, words that evoke the mental pictures they are seeing.

4 Play the listening three times.

5 Group the students in fours to compare the mental images they received.

6 Invite a few students to tell the whole class about their pictures.

What's the Most English Part?

Level	elementary to advanced
Materials	cassette / CD player, sheets of paper / notebooks

1 Write up on the board one or two phrases you feel are really very English in their expression and their feeling, phrases that are very different to the way the students' mother tongue works. For example, I might write up:

He goes, 'Why?'
She goes, 'Cos!'

To my mind the use of 'goes' instead of 'says' is very typical of current spoken UK English, as is the use of the present tense for reporting.

2 Ask the students to come up and write ways of saying things they find typically English all over the board.

3 Tell the students they are going to do a listening from their coursebook. Their task will be to pick out the two or three things they find most English and write them down. Tell them they will be able to listen to the text twice.

4 Play the listening twice.

5 Ask the students to write up what they have written on the board and then explain why they felt these were the most English things in the text.

6 Play the listening a third time.

NOTE: A useful way of getting students to do unstressed listening comprehension is to give them another task, in this case to listen to what seems to them most English. They do the listening comprehension as the secondary task and often end up doing it better as a result.

Choose My Best Voice

Level	elementary to advanced
Materials	none

1 Tell the students you are going to read them part of a passage from the coursebook in three different voices, and that they are to choose the one they like best.

2 For the first reading, stand in front of the group with your shoulders back and read in a fairly high voice and fairly fast so the people at the back can hear well. (You will be breathing from the upper part of your chest.)

3 Now sit in front of the group and read the same text in a slow, deep and fairly loud voice. Make your voice as resonant as you can and breathe from the pit of your stomach.

4 For the third reading, stand up and read the text in a lively, dramatic way with changes of speed and pitch.

5 Ask the students to tell you their preferred voice and why they liked that one best.

NOTE: As they do the task, the students are also doing anxiety-free listening comprehension.

Choose the Best Voice

Level	elementary to advanced
Materials	cassette / CD player, recordings of different voices

Preparation
Before the lesson, get three different native speakers of English to read a passage, or part of it, onto a cassette.

1 Ask the students to listen to the three readings on the cassette and tell them to choose the voice they like best for the reading of this text.

2 Ask the students to tell you which voice they prefer and why. At levels below elementary, this will need to happen in the mother tongue.

Four Ears Are Better Than Two

Level	lower intermediate to advanced
Materials	cassette / CD player, sheets of paper / notebooks

1 Choose a fairly long listening comprehension from the coursebook.

2 Play it to the students once and ask them to take notes of what they hear.

3 Ask them to go over their notes individually.

4 Pair the students and ask them to compare notes.

5 Ask them to form new pairs and compare notes again.

6 Play the listening a second time and ask the students to fill out their notes.

7 Tell the students to work with a new partner and tell them what new things they heard on the second listening.

8 Play the listening a third time, this time with the coursebooks open in front of them.

NOTE: Why should listening always be a lonely process? This activity socialises it.

Acknowledgement: I learnt this technique from Elisabeth Reber, at the May 2000 METU Conference in Turkey.

Text You Hear, Text You See

Level	elementary to upper intermediate
Materials	cassette / CD player, sheets of paper / notebooks, copies of listening transcript

Preparation
Photocopy the transcript for the listening text in the next unit. Make a copy of the **first half** of the transcript for each student. Do the same with the second half.

1 Give the first half of the transcript to a quarter of the students and send them out to read it in the corridor. Play the first half of the listening twice to the students left in the classroom.

2 Call the group of 'readers' back into the class. Group the students in fours so that one 'reader' now works with three 'listeners' and they use the transcript to puzzle out the meaning.

3 Play the listening a third time.

4 Repeat steps 1 to 3 again, this time sending out a different group of readers with the second half of the transcript.

5 Give out copies of both halves of the transcript to everybody who has not yet got them. Ask the students to read along silently, as you play the whole text.

6 Tell the students to turn over their transcripts and listen to the whole text without reading.

NOTE: This very visual way of doing listening comprehension is reassuring for those students whose strongest sensory channel is through their eyes.

Weed the Listening

Level	elementary to advanced
Materials	cassette / CD recorder, prepared transcript and recording

Preparation

Choose a transcript from a listening passage in the coursebook that is for one speaker. Insert between ten to fifteen wrong, superfluous words here and there. For example:

Change

'and she was walking up the steps when suddenly ...'

to

'and she was walking up the **because** steps when suddenly ... '

Get a friendly native speaker of English to rerecord the passage for you. It is vital that the adulterated passage be read confidently and fluently.

1 Say nothing to the students about what has been done. Play the listening and ask for the students' reactions.

2 Ask them to listen a second time and to write down all the superfluous words.

3 Ask the students to pool their words on the board.

4 Play the original listening and tell the students to add any other superfluous words to those on the board.

5 Play the false listening one last time.

Acknowledgement: This technique is used in one of the Cambridge CAE exam papers, and in *More Grammar Games* (Davis P et al, Cambridge, 1995). Here, it is adapted to listening.

Decoy Tasks to Help Listening

Level	elementary to lower intermediate
Materials	cassette / CD player, sheets of paper / notebooks

1 Tell the students they are going to hear a listening twice. Ask them to listen out for and jot down all the three- or four-syllable words they hear.

2 Ask the students to check their words with students sitting near them and play the listening again.

3 Tell them you are going to play the listening twice more and this time they are to listen out for and jot down all the irregular verbs.

4 Ask them which verbs they noticed and if they know all three parts of each verb.

5 The students check their results against the transcript in the coursebook.

6 Play the listening a fifth time.

Acknowledgement: Lonny Gold, writing in *Conference Proceedings*, SEAL, 1999, says of this activity, 'Since one of the ways of getting information into long-term memory is to make sure that it is perceived peripherally, the giving to students of an extraneous task to fulfil serves to occupy and sidetrack the conscious mind so the essential information reaches them unbeknownst.'

Doodling Listening Comprehension

Level	beginner to advanced
Materials	cassette / CD player, copies of transcript, sheets of paper / notebooks

Preparation

Make copies of the transcript of a listening from the coursebook.

1 Tell the students you will play the listening three times. Their task is to doodle on a piece of paper in as relaxed a way as they can.

2 After the three playings, group the students in fours. Tell them to compare their doodles and explain to each other what connections there are between the doodles and the parts of the text.

3 Give them the transcript to read silently.

4 Play the listening again and let them read along silently.

5 Ask the students to turn over the transcripts and listen to the text again.

NOTE: Doodling while listening is very useful for people who like multi-tasking. These people do one task better if they have another to work on simultaneously.

Acknowledgement: I learnt this activity from Adriana Díaz, a teacher in Argentina.

Beating the Rhythm of a Dialogue

Level	beginner to lower intermediate
Materials	cassette / CD player

1 Divide the class into groups. If there are three speakers, then you will have groups of three, if five speakers, then groups of five.

2 Tell the students to listen to the dialogue and raise their hands when their character is speaking.

3 Play the dialogue three times so each group becomes strongly associated with their speaker.

4 When you play the listening the fourth time, ask each group to tap out the rhythm of their speaker by clapping quietly.

5 Play it twice more so they really get involved in the clapping.

6 Ask the students to clap **and speak** along with their character three times.

NOTE: This exercise privileges those students who are strongly kinaesthetic, and who are sometimes the troublemakers in your class. It really keeps them happy!

Teacher Commentary on Text

Level	beginner to elementary (commentary in mother tongue), lower intermediate to advanced (commentary in English)
Materials	none

Preparation

Come to class ready to give your personal comments on the reading passage in the next unit. Think about what you are going to say, but don't write it down. For example, suppose this is the text:

If they made diving boards
six inches shorter,
think how much sooner
you'd be in the water.[1]

The commentary might run like this:

'A diving board ... that's one of those pieces of wood in a swimming pool. You jump from the diving board into the water. In fact, 'to dive' means to jump in head first.
Six inches ... how much is that in centimetres? I guess around sixteen to twenty cm.
I like the rhyme of 'shorter' and 'water'.
I like the word 'they'... it expresses so much about those parent-like people who decide for us, without asking us.
Just a minute ... how logical is this verse? Why on earth should shorter diving boards mean that you hit the water sooner? A **lower** diving board would mean this, not a **shorter** one.
OK, I get the picture ... the guy is standing on the six inch bit that has been cut off ... so he's in the water right away.'

Make your commentary on the passage standing in front of the class, but really talking to yourself.

NOTE: You are giving the students a model of reflective, inner-voice language that they do not get much of until they start reading literature in English.

Variation

After doing a number of commentaries yourself, group the students in sixes and ask a student in each group to give a commentary. (This can be in the mother tongue.)

Acknowledgement: I learnt this idea from Joanne Durham, a Pilgrims colleague in the summer of 2000.

[1] from *Grooks II*, Piet Hein Borgens Førlag

Snatches and Snippets

Level	beginner to lower intermediate
Materials	cassette / CD player, sheets of paper / notebooks

1 When dealing with a song in the coursebook, explain to the students that sometimes you want them to forget about doing 'listening comprehension'. Ask them to relax and just listen to the song with eyes shut and completely blank minds.

2 Play the listening a second time and ask the students to pick out any melody line, any sounds, any intonations, any vowels or consonants that they like. When the song is over, ask the students to replay the parts they liked in their own minds, silently or quietly.

3 Ask the students to share the things they like with the class.

4 Tell students to look at the transcript in the coursebook ask them to listen for declarative meaning.

NOTE: We teachers tend to forget the usefulness of apparent 'blank mind' listening, when the subconscious works unhampered by the conscious. Savouring language, once in a while, is just as important as understanding it.

Acknowledgement: This activity was inspired by a workshop given by Michelle Sadler, of the University of Washington.

7

Speaking

Many coursebooks offer a pronunciation syllabus and a series of structured and less structured activities to get students talking. The activities in this section are intended to complement those in the coursebook. In *Pronunciation* there are activities to help you to focus on the specific needs of your students, and *Keep Talking* looks at ways of keeping up the conversational flow.

Dealing with Hard Sound Patterns

Level	elementary to lower intermediate
Materials	sheets of paper / notebooks

Preparation
If you have students who find pronouncing consonant clusters hard and who find pronouncing final consonants difficult (the case with Thai learners, for example), then prepare a dictation in which they only take down the last three letters of each word dictated.

1 Tell the students you are going to give them a dictation, but they only need to take down the last three letters of each word. They leave dots for the omitted first letters.

2 Ask them to read back the sentences you have dictated, paying particular attention to clusters and to final vowels.

Variation
This dictation technique can be used to focus students' attention on particular sound problems. For example, if you teach initial 'h'-dropping Italians, then give them a different dictation, asking them to write down only the **first** three letters of each word. You need to prepare an 'h'-laden text. For example:

Henry had a huge appetite. He loved hamburgers and he sometimes ate herring. Now, in this hotel ...

Words People Mispronounce

Level	beginner to advanced
Materials	none

Preparation
Make a list of words your students typically mispronounce. For example:

independent
moonten (mountain)
bisquits (biscuits)
policeman
vumen (women)

1 Get the students up and moving. If the word you want them to practise is a four-syllable one, for example, 'independent', ask them to form lines of four.

2 Explain that each student is responsible for one syllable and the 'stressed syllable student' has their hands in the air over their head. Get different foursomes shouting out their syllables in sequence. The student representing the stressed syllable shouts louder and stamps their foot.

3 Now get students focusing on how the words are formed. Tell them to sit down again and mouth a word silently from your list. Ask them to identify the word.

4 Put some words from your list on the board. Pair the students and ask them to silently mouth the words to each other.

Acknowledgement: These techniques were proposed by Steve Norman in ENGLISH TEACHING *professional*, Issue 14, January 2000.

Stuttering Dictation

Level	elementary to lower intermediate
Materials	sheets of paper / notebooks

Preparation

Pick a paragraph or two from a previous unit of the coursebook. Prepare to stutter on certain sounds your students find hard because they are absent from their mother tongue. If you are working with Italians, for example, prepare to stutter on initial 'h' and on 'sm' and 'sn', etc. If you are working with Thai students, falter on consonant clusters like '**str**aight' and 'terri**ble**'.

1 Give the students your stuttering dictation.

2 Allow them to turn to the coursebook and correct any mistakes they have made.

3 Ask a few extrovert students to read the passage back to you, stuttering where you did, and thus emphasising the sounds they normally find hard.

Variation

If you want to focus attention on the pronunciation of vowels, then stammer when these come up.

NOTE: This is not a technique to use if you have a stutterer in the class.

Rods for Learning Stress Patterns

Level	beginner to lower intermediate (This activity is not practical with more than 25 students.)
Materials	a box of Cuisenaire rods

1 Ask the students to gather round a table so they can see easily.

2 Tell them they are going to hear an English word said once only, then one of them should demonstrate the word's stress pattern in rods. They should say it loudly and clearly and get the group to chorus it. (If you give them 'serious', a student might represent this as one tall rod and two little ones.)

3 Do this with words that follow the stress pattern/s the coursebook is currently dealing with.

Acknowledgement: I saw Simon Marshall use this technique from the Silent Way toolbox during a workshop at Pilgrims in the summer of 2000.

A Question not for Answering

Level	elementary to advanced
Materials	sheets of paper / notebooks

1 Ask each student to write down a question they do **not** want to answer about themselves. Assure them they **won't** have to answer it. Also ask them to write down a question they really **do** want to answer about themselves.

2 Get the students up and mingling. They have to find out how many people agree with them about the question they do **not** want to answer.

3 Group the students in sixes. Each person reads out the question they **would** like to answer and answers it at length.

Acknowledgement: I learnt this idea from Maria Eduarda Cardoso.

Throw a Ball and Talk

Level	elementary to upper intermediate
Materials	soft ball / ball made of newspaper

1 Stand or sit with your students in a circle.

2 Throw the ball to someone else in the circle and ask them a question.

3 The student with the ball answers the question then throws it to another student and asks them a question. Continue until many students have had a chance to speak.

4 Start a new round. This time, tell the student to throw the ball to a student who has already spoken and repeat what they said as accurately as possible. See how much they can remember.

5 Start a new round. This time, the student with the ball throws it and tells the catcher, 'I don't think you ...-ed yesterday', putting in an action she thinks the catcher did not do the previous day.

6 Start a new round. This time, the student with the ball compliments the student she throws it to.

7 In the last round, the student with the ball throws it to a student who has already spoken and repeats back accurately what they said.

NOTE: The two 'repeating back' rounds encourage students to listen carefully to each other.

Acknowledgement: These ideas were brainstormed in a teacher training workshop at TTI School, in Camden Town, London, UK.

Acting a Song or a Poem

Level	elementary to upper intermediate
Materials	none

1 Choose a song, poem or rhyme from the coursebook and ask the students to read it silently. Deal with any unknown words.

2 Ask the students to shut their eyes while you read it.

3 Tell them to open their eyes and read silently as you read the text aloud again.

4 Ask the students to stand up and read it aloud with you in chorus.

5 Tell them to mime and add gestures to go with the text. For example:

Hey Diddle Diddle,
The cat (pull a cat-like face) and the fiddle (mime playing a violin)
The cow jumped (mime jumping) over the moon (mime the moon in the sky)
The little boy laughed (mime guffawing) to see such fun
And the dish ran away (mime running) with the spoon (mime licking a spoon).

6 Get the students to mime and recite three times.

7 Tell them all to recite the text again three times, adding sounds to the mime. For example, in the nursery rhyme above, add a 'miaow' to the miming of the cat face, etc.

8 Tell the students to sit down again and ask them to work individually and change three things in the text. For example:

The cow jumped over the **sun**
The **big man cried** to see such fun
And the **fork** ran **back** with the **knife**

9 Invite some of the students read out some of their changes to the class.

Acknowledgement: I learnt this technical sequence from Bonnie Tsai at Pilgrims in the summer of 2000.

From Words to Dialogue

Level	beginner (This activity is for monolingual classes where you know their mother tongue.)
Materials	sheets of paper / notebooks

1 Choose a dialogue from your coursebook and write up six to ten key words or phrases. Check that the students understand them.

2 Get the class to chorus them in a whisper, in a loud voice, sadly, happily, etc.

3 Pair the students and ask them to write a dialogue using all the words and no others.

4 Get different pairs to act out their dialogue to the class.

5 Play the coursebook dialogue with the books shut, then tell the students to read the dialogue silently.

6 Play the dialogue again and tell students to read and listen. Ask them what parts of the dialogue they still have not understood.

Acknowledgement: I learnt this idea from Dave Allen at the Norwich Institute for Language Education, who got it from a colleague in Saudi Arabia whose name he has not retained.

Answering Questions While Marching

Level	beginner to lower intermediate
Materials	none

Preparation
Prepare to ask a series of questions that bring in language that has been covered in the last three or four units.

1 Ask the students to stand up and start marching on the spot. Get them going briskly. As they march, ask different students questions from your list.

2 When your questioning has finished and they have caught their breath, ask them what they noticed about marching on the spot and answering questions at the same time.

NOTE: Movement and oxygen intake are as vital in an adult class as with teenagers. All students bring bodies to class!

Rival Definitions

Level	lower intermediate to advanced
Materials	6-10 pieces of card, stopwatch

Preparation
Choose a set of six to ten words that need revising and put them each on a piece of card large enough for the whole class to see.

1 Ask for a volunteer team of five players.

2 Send three of the players out of the classroom, while one of the remaining two students faces the board with her back to the class.

3 Appoint a time-keeper with a stopwatch to time the game.

Game sequence
● Show the first word card, silently, to the whole class and to the fifth player.

● The fifth player runs to the fourth player by the board and quickly gives her a definition of the word. She tries to guess the word. If she can't, the fifth player gives her an expanded definition.

● The moment the fourth player has guessed correctly, she calls in the third player from outside and gives him a definition of the word, which he tries to guess as fast as he can.

● The third player then calls in the second player and gives her his definition of the word, and so on, until the last player has correctly guessed the word.

● The time-keeper announces the time that the first team took for their four members to guess the word from the various definitions offered.

4 Get a new group of five students to come out and play the game, this time with a new word. The time-keeper announces which of the first two teams was quickest and by how much.

5 Continue with new teams for each new word until all the words have been used up.

Acknowledgement: I saw this game on German TV, where they played female teams against male ones.

85

Talking to a Martian

Level	elementary to upper intermediate
Materials	none

Preparation
Select ten objects that are mentioned in the current unit of your coursebook.

1 Ask a student to volunteer to be a Martian, to whom everything has to be explained. Start with one of the ten objects. For example:

Volunteer: What's a 'lamp-post'?
You: Well, it gives light in the streets.
Volunteer: What's a 'street'?
You: A street? A long place between houses.
Volunteer: What's a 'house'?

2 Pair the students. Write the ten objects up on the board. Ask the students to have 'Martian' dialogues about each object. They take turns being the Martian.

Acknowledgement: This idea comes from the work of Paul Seligson.

Liar, Liar!

Level	elementary to advanced
Materials	none

Preparation
After you have spent some time on narrative tenses, ask your students to come to the next class with a story to tell about themselves. Explain that it can be a true story or an invention.

1 Group the students in sixes and ask each student to tell their story without saying whether it is fact or fiction.

2 After each telling, get the students to vote on whether the story is true or invented. The teller says nothing. When all six people have told their stories, the tellers reveal if they lied or told the truth.

Variation
Andrew Wright suggests that if you have to set your student an essay subject like 'My Last Summer Holidays', you can spice it up by asking the students to each include three untruths. When the essays have been written, you get the students working in fours reading each other's compositions. Their task is try to spot the lies.

Acknowledgement: This idea was proposed by Yvonne Castino in the October 2000 issue of ENGLISH TEACHING *professional*.

How Do You Get Out of Bed?

Level	lower intermediate to advanced
Materials	chalk or markers for the board, sheets of paper / notebooks

This is a good activity to get students going on a Monday morning.

1 Ask some or all the students to come to the board. Have them all lined up ready with chalk or markers before you tell them what they are to draw.

2 Tell them to draw something to represent 'getting up in the morning'.

3 Tell the students to go and sit down. Give yourself time to look at the drawings carefully, and then ask, 'Whose is this?', pointing to a particular drawing. Ask, 'How does this person feel?' As you look at different drawings, you will wonder about different things. Ask the students about them.

4 Give the students this dictation:

Getting Out of Bed Dictation
Is waking up a happy moment in the day for me?
How, exactly, do I wake up? How long does it take?
Typically, what is the first thing I pay proper attention to?
On waking, do I think about the day ahead or about yesterday?
How much time passes between my waking up and my getting out of bed?
How, physically, do I get out of bed? Is it a slow process or a fast one?
How much are memories of my dreams with me after getting up?
Has my getting up changed over time? Did it use to be different from now?
If I think back, which have been my most memorable awakenings?

5 Group the students in fours and get them to answer the questions.

Stories from Objects

Level	lower to upper intermediate
Materials	objects supplied by students

Preparation
Choose a unit where lots of small objects are mentioned. For example, ' comb', 'pen', 'spoon', 'penknife', 'bottletop', etc. Ask the students to bring in between six and a dozen of these objects each.

1 Pair the students. Ask them to pool their objects and to each choose one that could have a story told about it. Student A then tells student B the 'story' of their object. The story can be as wild as they like. Student B then tells student A a wild story about their object.

2 Student A now tells student B a more likely story about student B's object. Student B does the same, focusing on student A's object.

3 Tell the students to get up and mingle. They should each find a new partner and tell the story they like best from the previous two exchanges.

Acknowledgement: I met this technique in a workshop at the SEAL Conference in the spring of 2001.

Phrases I Like, Phrases I Hate

Level	elementary to advanced (At elementary level, the mother tongue will be used.)
Materials	photocopies of a reading text

1 Ask students to work on their own and underline four phrases, words or clauses they like in a reading passage.

2 In turn, each student reads out an underlined item.

3 Ask the students to explain **why** they like it. Some students will underline the same phrases, but often for different reasons.

Variations

a The students underline four things they dislike in the reading passage.

b Ask half the students to underline four things they like and half to underline four things they dislike. (This will often produce a clash of perceptions / opinions.)

Acknowledgement: I learnt this from Lonny Gold, a suggestopaedic teacher working in Paris.

Picture Preview

Level	lower intermediate to advanced
Materials	sheets of paper / notebooks

1 After you have done the first couple of units in the book, write this questionnaire up on the board:
  - Which picture in this book has the most attractive colour/s?
  - Which picture has the deepest perspective?
  - Which has the most interesting lines?
  - Which has the most interesting use of shadow?
  - Which is the clearest?
  - Which picture do you like best?
  - Which is most boring?
  - Which one do you think I like best?

2 Explain the technical words so everybody understands 'perspective', 'lines', 'clearest', 'shadow', etc.

3 For homework, ask the students to look at all the pictures in the book and answer the questionnaire.

4 In the next class, group the students in fours or fives to feed back to each other on how they judge the pictures.

5 Ask them to guess your own opinion of the visuals. Tell them what you really think.

8

Looking Backwards and Forwards

Most coursebooks are leading implicitly or explicitly towards an exam, and are structured to allow for revision and consolidation. Looking backwards and forwards is something that students need to do frequently. Here are some ideas for going back over students' coursework and building their confidence for approaching exams.

Confidence-boosting Reformulation

Level	elementary to advanced
Materials	sheets of paper / notebooks

Preparation
Pick out the weakest composition in the class and prepare to reformulate it so it becomes one of the best.

Dictate the composition, minus the mistakes, to the whole class.

Acknowledgement: Luke Prodromou, in an article in *IATEFL Issues*, August - September 2000, writes about this technique: 'The whole idea of recycling is a powerful metaphor when dealing with error: by recycling we give new life to the students' work; we send out a message that nothing is wasted, nothing is worthless. We get maximum input from the students' own imperfect efforts - our task is to piece out their imperfections with a positive frame of mind and a belief in the value of all students' contributions.'

Dictating Mistakes

Level	elementary to advanced
Materials	sheets of paper / notebooks

Preparation
Drawing on the students' written homework, prepare a set of sentences to dictate, some of them with the students' errors in them and some of them with the students' errors corrected.

1 Before giving the students their homework back, explain that you are going to dictate some of their sentences. Half will be correct and half will be wrong.

2 Pair the students. Tell them to decide after each sentence if it is correct or if it needs correcting and, if so, how.

3 Dictate the sentences and leave the pairs time for discussion after each one.

4 Let the students tell you what they have decided and why. You may find out interesting things about their language thinking. At the end of the feedback, make sure everybody knows what is right and what is wrong.

5 Give back their homework.

NOTE: Please don't use this exercise if you think showing students flawed language is dangerous. I think it is fine as long as they know it may be flawed.

Acknowledgement: You will find a version of this activity in *Grammar Games* (Rinvolucri M, Cambridge, 1985), plus a few more of the same sort that invite students to think for themselves.

Throw a Ball and Translate

Level	beginner to advanced (Students must share same mother tongue.)
Materials	soft ball / ball made with newspaper

Preparation
Choose any set of words from the previous units and ask the students to learn them for homework. You could choose numbers at beginner level, frequent grammar words like 'and', 'but', 'because', 'although', 'never' at lower intermediate level, or complex lexical chunks or collocational pairs at advanced level.

1 Ask the students to sit or stand in a circle.

2 Tell the first student to throw a ball to one of their classmates and say a word from your revision list to the student who catches it. This student then shouts out the translation in their mother tongue and throws the ball to someone else, calling out another word from the revision list, etc.

Variation
Instead of using a revision list, you could run this exercise freely. The student with the ball shouts out any English word and the recipient of the ball has to give a mother tongue equivalent. New English words thrown up this way go up on the board for consolidation work after the ball game is over.

Acknowledgement: This idea was generated during a teacher training brainstorm at TTI School in Camden, London.

Word, Definition, Example Sentences

Level	elementary to advanced
Materials	grid on A3 paper with 30 words written on it, five counters

Preparation
Give the class a list of thirty words taken from previous units to revise for homework.

On a sheet of A3 paper, draw a grid with five columns and six rows like this:

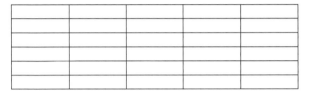

Write the thirty words into the thirty boxes. Make five counters labelled A - E.

1 Divide your class into five teams. Each team is given a counter marked with their letter: 'A', 'B', 'C', 'D' or 'E'.

2 Explain the game:
- Team A can start with any word in the left-hand column. They put their counter over that word square and give a definition of the word plus an example. If you think all is correct, they stay on their square. If not, they move off the board.
- Team B then puts their counter on another word in the left-hand column, etc.
- The teams move across the board from left to right. When they move from column 1 to column 2, they can go for the word diagonally up from them, diagonally down or the one horizontally next to them.
- The winning team is the one that first manages to reach column 6, the right-hand column.

3 Make sure the game goes at a brisk pace and only accept or reject definitions and sentences. **Don't** offer definitions yourself.

4 After the game is over, go back over any serious language misconceptions.

Placing Words in a Street

Level	elementary to advanced
Materials	none

1 Ask your students to bring to mind a street they know very well. They describe their street or road to a partner.

2 Give them twenty to twenty-five words from the coursebook unit / units that you hope they will revise. Check they remember the meanings of all the words.

3 Ask the students to close their eyes and mentally place each of the words in the street or the space near it. Give them five minutes for this.

4 Group the students in fours and ask them to describe to the others where they have mentally placed the words, and why.

Acknowledgement: In *Vocabulary* (Morgan et al, Oxford, 1986), you will find an exercise where students draw their flat / house ground-plan and write words on it.

First and Last Letter Dictation

Level	elementary to lower intermediate
Materials	sheets of paper / notebooks

1 Choose a reading passage that you worked on three to four weeks ago.

2 Dictate between three and four paragraphs of it and ask the students to write down only the first and last letters of each word, leaving an appropriate space in between.

3 Group the students in threes and ask each student in the group to read the text to the other two.

Acknowledgement: This dictation idea comes from the set of Gurdjieff practical exercises, to be found in *On Love and Psychological Exercises* (Orage A R, Samuel Weiser, 1998).

Changing the Time Standpoint

Level	elementary to advanced
Materials	pieces of string (one for every 2 students), envelopes (1 for each student), sheets of paper

1 At the end of the term or course, randomly pair the students. Hold up a bunch of pieces of string. There should be one string to every two students. Ask each student to take the end of a piece of string. Let go of the strings and people are paired!

2 Give each student an envelope on which they write their own address. Ask them to give the envelope to their partner, but do not sit with him or her.

3 Ask each student to imagine that they are now two months into the future, looking back over eight weeks to the end of the term / course. Ask them to put the date, two months ahead, on their letter. Tell them to write a letter to their partner about the term / course, looking back from this future standpoint.

4 When the students have finished writing and have put the letters in the envelopes, collect them and have the school office post them.

Acknowledgement: The idea of writing back from a point in the future was suggested by a Norwegian Science teacher, Elin Oknes.

Pattern Sentences on the Hoof

Level	beginner to lower intermediate
Materials	none

1 Get your students into an open space where they can move.

2 Give the students an example sentence of the grammar you have taught them.

3 Give them these commands:
- Walk forwards
- Freeze (they freeze and say the sentence to students near them)
- Walk backwards (they do so without bumping into others)
- Freeze, speak sadly (they say the pattern sentence sadly)
- Freeze, whisper (they whisper the sentence to students nearby, and so on).

4 Give them a new example sentence for the grammar you have taught and give them some more movement practice.

NOTE: The focus on moving and not banging into people distracts the conscious mind from the grammar and allows it to be absorbed unconsciously. This is a wonderful exercise for very kinaesthetic students.

Exam Confidence Letters

Level	elementary to advanced
Materials	envelopes (1 for each student), sheets of paper

1 About three weeks before an important exam, give each student an envelope and ask them to write a letter to themselves that they will open on the day of the exam. Ask the students to address the envelopes to themselves and state the place, date, day of the week and time of day, at the head of the letter.

2 Tell them to write 'Dear ...' and their name, and sign it. Explain that the letter is entirely private. No one but them will see it.

3 In the letter they should write about times when they have done an exam well, and wish themselves good questions and good luck.

4 Tell them they have fifteen minutes in which to write the letter. They then put it in the envelope and seal it.

5 Take in all the letters.

6 Give each student their envelope back on the day of the exam.

Acknowledgement: I learnt the application of the 'letter to self' idea to exam confidence-building, from Gary Collins, KV Reinach, Switzerland.

Exams I Have Enjoyed

Level	elementary to advanced
Materials	none

1 Come to class prepared to tell the story of an exam you enjoyed, for whatever reason. Tell your story.

2 Get the students up and mingling. Tell them to find a person who can tell them the story of an exam they enjoyed.

3 Ask a student to come and write one story they heard on the board.

4 Lightly underline the places in the text where there are mistakes. Get the class to suggest alternatives.

NOTE: This exercise is especially useful for students who do not believe that they (or anybody else!) could possibly enjoy an exam.

Sharing Pre-exam Feelings

Level	elementary to advanced
Materials	sheets of paper / notebooks

1 Write up these sentence stems and ask each student to complete them:

- Three months before an exam, I feel ...
- Three weeks before an exam, ...
- The way I revise in the last week is ...
- Just before going into the examination hall, ...
- I use the first few minutes of the exam to ...
- I use the last half hour of the exam to ...
- After an exam, typically I feel ...

2 Group the student in fives or sixes. Ask them to share their sentence endings with each other.

NOTE: Realising that other students, sometimes apparently self-confident ones, also have tensions and worries in the exam area, can be a great relief. A worry shared is a worry halved.

Speed Writing

Level	elementary to advanced
Materials	sheets of paper

1 Check that all the students have pen and paper ready.

2 Ask them to stand up and run on the spot for about ninety seconds. Get them going hard, so that their breathing changes.

3 Tell the students that they have a timed ninety seconds to write as much as they can (in meaningful sentences) about a topic (for example, 'yesterday', 'uncles', 'driving tests', etc.). Say that you will give a prize to the student who has written the most words.

4 They should write for exactly ninety seconds. They must stop writing the second you tell them to.

5 Tell the students to correct their texts for silly slips, then count their words, so a winner emerges.

6 Group the students in fours to listen to each other's texts.

NOTE: Ninety seconds of speed writing in the examination, to get one's mind moving in the direction of writing a composition, is much better than ten minutes of biro-end-chewing. The speed writing is simply to get ideas moving and to gear oneself up. Not all students find the technique helpful. I would do half a dozen speed writing bouts before an important written exam, so students can judge for themselves if it will be useful to them on the day.

Students Write the Class Tests

Level	elementary to advanced
Materials	copies of reading text and amended text

Preparation
Once your class has got used to the types of test proposed by the coursebook, you can reduce the tedium of class tests by asking the students to produce their own. Cloze tests can be widely used for this.

Give half the class a copy of the reading text and tell them that, for homework, they have to rewrite it, omitting every sixth word. Give the other half of the class the same text, but with an extra paragraph added on. For homework, they rewrite it, omitting every seventh word.

1 Tell the students to do the cloze test prepared by the students in the other half of the class. They should give their test paper to someone in the other half of the class to mark.

2 Collect the marks and adjust them so they are fair (there may be more gaps to be filled in one cloze test than in the other).

NOTE: This technique is based on the ideas in Sheelagh Deller's *Lessons from the Learner* (Pilgrims-Longman, 1990). Sheelagh thinks teachers waste too much time doing 'busy work', and endless marking of class tests is very much busy work. In this classic exercise, the students prepare for their own test while preparing a test for others. They consolidate their learning while marking their classmate's test. And you have more time in the evening for intelligent thinking.

professional
perspectives

professional perspectives is a series of practical methodology books designed to provide teachers of English with fresh insights, innovative ideas and original classroom materials. It is published by DELTA PUBLISHING.

Other titles in the series include:

The Resourceful English Teacher
by Jonathan Chandler and Mark Stone
A complete teaching companion containing over 200 classroom activities for use in a wide range of teaching situations

Creating Conversation in Class
by Chris Sion
More than 100 imaginative ideas and stimulating activities designed to get students talking in class

The MINIMAX Teacher
by Jonathan Taylor
Practical, easy-to-use activities that generate the maximum student output from the minimum teacher input

Using the Mother Tongue
by Sheelagh Deller and Mario Rinvolucri
Ready-to-use activities which make creative use of the students' mother tongue in the language learning classroom

For a full list and further details of titles in the *professional perspectives* series, contact the publishers at:

DELTA PUBLISHING
Quince Cottage
Hoe Lane
Peaslake
Surrey GU5 9SW
England

Tel +44 (0)1306 731770
E-mail info@deltapublishing.co.uk
Web www.deltapublishing.co.uk